BLACK AXE

FALL'

By S. Jonas Black

'LET THE BLACK AXE FALL'

Preface

For those of you who are not familiar with my other books, this introduction will tell you a little more about myself. For those of you who have read any of my other books, you probably already know why I write under the pseudonym of 'S Jonas Black', please bear with me as I explain what you probably already know about me and the pseudonyms I use in my writing.

I have a 'YouTube' show as well as an on-line blog that focuses mainly on Government cover-ups and theories on other conspiracies. I usually allow almost any discussion, however, sometimes I focus on topics whereby I need to protect the sources and other innocent people who risk so much to bring their stories not only to me but to you too. This started with the three documents I disclosed in my first book, 'The Trifecta Papers'. It is for this reason that I use my pseudonym of 'S. Jonas Black' for these publications. As the safety of those who trust me with the information that they have provided to me will always be my primary concern, I will always take great steps to ensure that the anonymity of my informants is strictly kept. I take other steps to ensure their safety, some I have disclosed, and other steps I will keep to myself, for more information on these safety steps, please read 'The Trifecta Papers'.

When I wrote my last book, 'The Canadian French Affair' (later renamed 'How I was used by the Sûreté and the CIA'); I told the reader about an RCMP officer named 'Steven Browne' (again a pseudonym). During my interviews with this officer for my previous book, I learned his story of how he began his work with the RCMP Special I office. It was fascinating to listen to what was told to me, and I hope I reflected it as accurately as possible as his story is worth retelling. As this is his true story (of course once again his name has been changed for his protection and anonymity), there is no climax point like you would find in most action novels. That is because this is his true account on how a seemingly simple police call turned into something much bigger than it first seemed. This book, unlike my others, is not a detail on a conspiracy (except for the criminal group called 'Black Axe'), instead it is 'Steven Browne's' account of his investigation that must be protected. Therefore, in addition to his name, the location of his deployments within in the RCMP are also fictitious. In fact, all the names within this book are made up to protect those who were involved in investigations of these crimes.

There still is a conspiracy of course, but not from the RCMP or government agency unlike most of my podcasts, YouTube videos and books. This is the conspiracy on how a world-wide criminal organization targets people to obtain potentially huge sums of money. Truthfully, I am more concerned of backlash from 'Black Axe' than I am from any government agency. I sincerely hope you enjoy reading it as much as I enjoyed researching and writing it. It is for this reason that I also change the names of all the other people involved throughout this book. Their names may be fake, but this story of theirs is not. Also, it is entirely possible that the criminal organization called 'Black Axe' may have a nefarious interest in this officer, so naturally I want to protect him. But it has always been my policy to not only change the names of everyone in my books, but where possible to change the locations of the events as well.

Sure, this book is more about an investigation into a criminal group than it is a government conspiracy situation or cover-up like all my other publications, but I thought his story is so compelling that I feel it needs to be told. The reason his story needs to be heard is two-fold; first, it is very interesting how he discovered and investigated a major crime ring; secondly, it is his hope that knowing what had happened to others, maybe someone else will be protected from on line scams in the future. There is of course a criminal conspiracy here (or I likely would not be writing this book), but unlike the usual conspiracies I write about, this one is not from the government or military at all. This is a conspiracy from an extremely organized group of criminals who work closely together, yet at the same time, spread apart worldwide, to scam lonely people out of their money. And in doing so, they have hurt countless people. Not just financially, but emotionally too. This has resulted in many shattered lives as well as many suicides and other devastation. These scammers have no regard for the lives of others. They are the equivalent to a drug addict simply concerned with obtaining their next fix. In fact, I would bet most drug addicts have more remorse and feelings then these monsters have.

In addition to Steven Browne wanting to tell his story, it is also my sincere hope that by reading this book, someone somewhere will be protected from an internet romance scam from what they have learned in reading this account. I also believe it is important for anyone who is looking for love on the internet to know how these scams are done. That is why at the end of this book I list things to look for, what to do if you find them, and how to protect yourself. The criminals are hoping their victims feel extreme shame over their belief in these people, that way very few reports are ever given to the law enforcement officials. That is exactly why I am asking any victim of this type of crime to report it to the police. Even if it seems there is little that can be done; documenting it and making our lawmakers in the nation's Capital aware of what is occurring, can save not only others from being victims, but it can save their lives too. Also, it could promote romance and dating websites to set up better ways to prevent these scammers from preying on their victims.

It never ceases to amaze me how a seemingly simple call for a police officer to take, can end up resulting in exposing a major crime or crime spree by an organized criminal organization that not only spans the second largest country in the world, but an organization so vast that their criminal exploits cover many countries in most continents. It may not be a routine occurrence, but it sure does happen. If only there was an easy way for the police working routine patrol to know when these matters would become a sign of a huge underlying crime. This is an example of an officer whose curiosity, from being very new on the force, had caused him to uncover something very big from a call that initially looked very routine and in fact most officers would have treated it as just that, a routine call not worthy of any extra investigation.

I should point out that when this investigation occurred, the common email protocol of the time was POP3 whereby you would log on to the internet and download your email onto your computer which then removes it from the server and stores it on your computer. That is how the emails were traced as you will read on in this book. Today the technology is different, but this did happen a few years ago.

As I have stated in my previous books, it is always my hope that in the future I will be able to bring more of these important accounts and stories forward. If you are aware of any stories that you believe the government is covering up, or that anonymity is needed, please feel free to bring them to my attention. I would love to cover them in my books. And as I have stated many times in the past, I will always make your safety and security my number one priority when I receive information from you.

Thank you and I hope you like this book. Please feel free to contact me at the email address listed here as well as my Facebook page. I may be slow to respond, but I will endeavour to reply to all tips for stories and answer whatever questions I can reasonable respond to.

Thank you,

S Jonas Black

Email: sjonasblack@gmail.com

Facebook: S Jonas Black

Chapter one

In my previous book, 'The Canadian - French Affair', the readers were introduced to the many officers involved in the investigation. There was the main person who worked for the 'Communications Security Establishment' (CSE), the CIA, and the Sûreté and of course there were members of the RCMP. There was one RCMP officer in particular, to whom I assigned the fictitious name of 'Steven Browne'. Since the time frame of that investigation, Corporal Steven Browne has secured a transfer back to British Columbia which was the province he was born and grew up in. He is still working in Special I section, but now it is at the 'E Division' with their now headquarters located in Surrey British Columbia (at the time of this investigation, E Division was located in the city of Vancouver).

One time I was visiting my good friend John Robinson (also a pseudonym I assigned to him to use in my book 'The Canadian French Affair' later rereleased with the new name 'How I was used by the Sûreté and the CIA'). He now resides in Vancouver where he moved shortly after he retired. I was visiting with him when I was fortunate enough to have an opportunity to sit down once again with Steven Browne during that same trip. It was on this occasion, when I was interviewing Steven, that he told me of a time when he first started on routine patrol duties as a rookie constable in Prince George. He had come straight out of Depot in Regina only a short time before this incident took place. His account intrigued me so much I felt it should be put in print. This is his account of what occurred as it was told to me. What should have started out as a routine 'Break and Enter' call and report resulted in an investigation conducted by Constable Steven Browne, ended up being a call that took him in a direction no one ever thought this call would lead him. What he eventually uncovered was the most remarkable discovery that a new police officer could ever hope for, or wish he never took that call in the first place. Here is his story as it occurred several years ago;

Steven was only one day away from his graduation ceremony from the Royal Canadian Mounted Police (RCMP) training center in Regina Saskatchewan. The past few months seemed both long and short at the same time. It was a paradox that few would understand. Long at the beginning, as the end seemed so far away, and the course load was hard with tough instructors who demanded the best from you. And short, as that time really did pass quickly. He was already made aware of where his first posting would be. He would be working in Prince George in the province of British Columbia for his one year of on the job field training. But that was still a couple weeks away. As for right now, he was busy polishing his tall brown boots and ensuring that his uniform was looking very sharp and crisp for the big ceremony tomorrow afternoon.

Both his parents had traveled to Regina to be there at the graduation ceremony for their son. They were both so proud of his accomplishments. Tonight, he would have time to join them for an early celebratory dinner, but he still needed to ensure that all his kit looked to be at it's finest for tomorrow's big day. As for now, he wanted to finish up all his tasks in time for the dinner tonight with his mom and dad whom he has not seen for several months. He had been here in Regina at Depot for some time, and although the training staff kept him very busy, Steven still had enough time to think about the family and friends he missed back home. Some of them would make the trip to Regina to be there on his big day, just as his parents had done for him. Others simply sent their best wishes and words of encouragement.

He met his parents at the restaurant they chose in downtown Regina. It was a very nice steak house that his father knew they would all enjoy. Besides, it was at a convenient location approximately halfway between the hotel and the RCMP Depot. Entering the restaurant, Steven's mom spotted him first and came up to him and wrapped her arms around her son who she had not seen for several months. His dad shook his hand vigorously and gave him an early congratulations for completing his police recruit training. They sat down and talked about all the training he had undergone, and all the exacting things that Steven learned since day one at Depot. They talked about his future and what his goals are within the RCMP. Steven explained to his parents that within the RCMP, he was not really finished his training yet, just the classroom part of his training. He still needed one year of field training and this would take place at the Prince George detachment. During this time, he would be doing primarily general duties. But he would also spend some time with various sections learning a small amount of their innumerable duties too.

He would be spending time with the traffic section, which really interested him. He would spend a shift or two with the dog handers section, and this also sounded like it would be interesting. He mentioned to his dad that this may be the area of policing for him as he always loved dogs and plans to get one or two when he settles into his permanent home in the future. Other sections he would be joining would be accident investigations, drug sections, and so many more. Working in the community police office, giving security advise to the public, was not high on his list to do, but he knew it was a section that had to be staffed and he would have to do his turn at it as well.

His Parents enjoyed listening to him talk about the different things he would get to do during his first year. The two of them could hear the excitement in Steven's voice as he told them all about it. They both had a huge respect for their son who would be proudly wearing the uniform of Canada's national police agency. But above all else, they were happy for Steven having accomplished his goals to become a police officer with the Royal Canadian Mounted Police. They couldn't be any happier for him and proud of who he had become as an adult.

After hearing about all that Steven had done in the past few months, his parents brought him up to date on all the things going on with his extended family and friends. Steven enjoyed hearing about all of them, he had not had too much contact with them over the past few months as he was kept very busy in all his training. It was so good to catch up on all this. Up to now it was just through emails and he only had the time to give brief responses to them.

After a long dinner followed by a nice dessert and a coffee, Steven had to say goodbye to his parents for the night, but he did comment that he looked forward to seeing them after the graduation ceremony the following day. There would be coffee served as well as hors d'oeuvres after the ceremony at which point, he could spend some more time socializing with them.

He proceeded back to the depot to see that many of his troop mates were still up and working on their uniforms while talking in the barracks common area. So, Steven retrieved his boots and his brown shoe polish and joined them there too. Coincidently the television show 'COPS' was on the TV and they were all watching and laughing while they were talking and getting their kit looking it's best.

The recruits had awakened very early even though it was their last day, but this was because the mess hall had set hours for their breakfast. That morning they did one last rehearsal for the graduation ceremony. It was early that afternoon when the ceremony took place. The drill hall was filled with family and friends, and of course there were the dignitaries and the reviewing officer. Steven looked sharp in his red serge and his Stetson-style hat. The troop marched on to the parade square and the audience was thrilled to see family and friends graduate from their long and difficult training. Steven had wanted to be a police officer for many years, and the past few months was a culmination of hard work, dedication, and seeing his dream become his reality.

Today he would get to celebrate his achievement with his family, his friends, and all the acquaintances he met while at depot. But it was bittersweet to him. He made many good friends and he knew that for many of them, this would be the last time he would ever get to see them. Tomorrow, he would leave Depot early in the morning to begin his long drive to Prince George to start the second part of his police training, the field training component. He knew that for the coming year, he would be graded by the officers who have already been put through the paces he will be put through. But he looked forward to this next step in his training, albeit with a nervous excitement.

The ceremony was very nice and after the reception at the end, he said goodbye to his friends and family. The next morning, he would be on his way to his first assignment.

Steven had always loved to go on long drives, and this drive was no different. The weather was nice, and he enjoyed the solitude too. So, he said goodbye to Regina and headed west to his new adventure and his new career.

During the drive, he wondered to himself what exciting things he will be involved in. He wondered what his very first arrest will be. (It turned out to be a DIPP arrest – Drunk in Public Place). What will the other officers be like at his first detachment? Although all these questions went through his mind, he never deterred from the excitement he felt. Every time he passed a police officer in their RCMP car on the highway on route to Prince George, he had to remind himself that he too is now one of them.

Steven started the field part of his career with his black patrol boots polished to an immaculate shine and his creases on the uniform that he proudly wore, were sharp and crisp. Since he was a child, the dream of someday being a Mountie was always at the forefront of his desire for a career. He had visions when he was a little boy of protecting the innocent, catching the guilty, and making everything safer for everyone. When he got older, he also got wiser, knowing that it is much easier to dream this, than it was for him to succeed at this. But his hard work to get in, and then pass his depot training had paid off, he was now a full-fledged police officer.

His initial few days in Prince George was used for showing him around the station, introducing him to the other officers, and a new partner taking him out to go on calls and show him around the city he would call home for the next year. Steven felt a sense of pride that he had never experienced before and was enjoying all the new and exciting things he would experience during this year.

Here he was now, just a few weeks out of depot when he showed up for work on the start of a four-day rotation. Today he would be working by himself in a car, taking calls on his own. He worked from six in the morning to six in the evening for two days, followed by two days of six in the evening to six in the morning for two days. This rotation, although fair to all general duty members, did take some getting used to as the shifts raised havoc on a body's internal clock. But Steven was beginning to get used to this new routine that he might have to do for several years to come.

After the morning rollcall and daily briefing session, Steven went to his patrol car that was parked out back of the station from the previous officer who used it. It was here in the police parking lot that he began his daily pre-check of his assigned car before getting out on the road. The precheck consisted of a comprehensive walk-around of the car to ensure that any damage is noted, and any new damage is reported to a supervisor before the vehicle is removed from the parking lot. Included in the precheck is a look under the hood to ensure that all the belts look good, lights work, and fluids levels are fine. Finally, you search the prisoner compartment in the back seat of the patrol car to ensure that the last prisoner didn't hide a weapon or any other contraband in there that a subsequent prisoner could find. Officer safety is always the primary concern and it should never be taken lightly.

Steven remembered the instructors telling him back in Regina that it is not uncommon to find your car filled with sunflower seed shells and MacDonald's garbage located on the floor of the front of the police car. But so far, he has been fortunate to have never had that issue. The worst he found so far was a used MacDonald's coffee cup lid that was obviously missed which the last officer failed to notice when cleaning out his own garbage.

Once Steven was satisfied that the patrol car was good to go for his shift and that there was nothing hidden in the back seat prisoner compartment, he logged on to the on-board computer and sent a message to the dispatcher that he was now 'in service' and able to take calls. He took a quick glance at his fuel gauge to confirm that he was left with a full tank of gas from the previous officer. Sadly, this curtesy did not always occur. Sometimes it was returned near empty, but when possible, it should always be returned with at least a half a tank of gas, but preferably a full tank. He knew he was good to go on the road without any fuel concerns.

The on-board computer in police cars will show a list of all the calls that are pending, or ones that currently have an officer assigned to it. The computer was a Panasonic Toughbook that could be removed from the vehicle mount and used remotely from its built-in battery. This allows the officer to work on reports without the need to be sitting in the patrol car to type. Often, they would bring them into coffee shops to finish off reports. Likely these computers had coffee spilled on them from time to time and the keyboards likely had many crumbs. These computers were really tough like their name implies.

Steven was scanning the list of pending calls on the computers screen to see what was close by. He noticed that there was one call coming from an area far north of Prince George on route to a more remote area called 'Summit Lake'. Steven didn't really want to take that call, as it would be a long drive to get there, for what would likely be a routine break and enter report followed by the long drive back to Prince George. It would probably result in a long report but nothing else. But sometimes this can be a nice way to spend two or three hours too. However, Steven still being new and keen, he wanted something a little more challenging and exciting than what was probably a boring and routine break and enter report at a summer cabin. The break-in could have been a month ago for all he or the cabin owner knew. Break in's on cabins often do not get discovered until long after they occur as the owners sometimes do not visit their cabins for many months at a time.

Before he even left the police parking lot, he became the officer that the dispatcher had assigned to go on this call. His first reaction was disappointment. He wondered if he got this call because he was considered the 'rookie' constable on his first posting at this detachment. He didn't complain though, and instead he decided to make the best of it. He did like going for long drives and this would give him that opportunity. Knowing it would be a longer drive, he thought to himself about getting an extra-large cup of Tim Horton's coffee at a local drive through before his drive north. Maybe with some luck, he could stop a few violators on the highway to make the trip a little more productive than what was likely to be a single simple report. Catching an excessive speeder was commonplace if you looked for them. But today Steven would be only catching the ones he wouldn't have to park his car and clock their speed for. Also, as it was an overcast day with a just light dusting of snow on the ground, it would be less likely to find people driving too fast.

After going through the Tim Horton's drive through and picking up his usual morning coffee and muffin, He pulled out to highway 97 and headed north towards the holding break and enter call. The sun would not come up for more than one hour. As there was also a light dusting of fresh snow on the ground, people were driving safely for the most part, but the roads were bare and sanded to make them considerably safer. Steven had always assumed the streets were slick with ice to keep a safe attitude. The overcast clouds provided the occasional snowflake falling from the sky, but it was so little it didn't amount to anything substantial and the visibility would likely be great once the sun came up. There were very few vehicles on the highway that Steven saw at this early time of the morning, as it wasn't even seven o'clock yet. The few cars he did see were likely ones heading south to Prince George who were probably making their way in to work, and these drivers were, for the most part, driving very responsibly. Sometimes the perception of bad road conditions could actually make things safer as people acted smarter behind the wheel. Sadly though, this theory didn't always hold true and there were some catastrophic accidents as a result.

    Coincidently there are several lakes called 'Summit Lake' scattered throughout British Columbia, but this specific one with that name is situated approximately fifty kilometers north of Prince George. In the early part of the last century, it served as an important transportation hub, being situated on the Arctic Divide. The 'Crooked River' flows north from Summit Lake to the Parsnip and Peace rivers and then on to the Arctic Ocean far to the North.

After some time driving north, a trip that Steven actually enjoyed making, he arrived at the address that was shown on his computer screen, he was also aided by the GPS on his on-board computer, this also allowed the dispatcher to follow where he was driving. His timing was good considering the road conditions and that it was still dark outside. He arrived in just under one hour, and in the east, he could see the sky starting to get a little lighter. In about half an hour the sun would be up enough to see the area properly.

In the summertime, it would have been a much quicker drive, but at this time of the year, the roads had the possibility of being very icy and there was no need to go faster than the winter road conditions would safely allow. After exiting his patrol car, he walked to the front door of the cabin indicated on his car computer. An older gentleman met him at the door to tell him he had arrived at his cabin the previous evening and found his door broken and that someone had gained entry into the building. This type of incident on its own was not unusual in any way. These kinds of break-ins are relatively commonplace for cabins in remote parts. Sometimes it was from a traveling person or a homeless person looking for a dry place to stay, or to see if there was anything worth stealing that could be sold for some quick cash.

It was obvious at first glance that the door jam and striker plate was not very strong to begin with, and it broke with likely nothing more than a good hard shove. Steven asked if there was anything stolen from inside the cabin. The older man reported to him that the only things missing was some canned food that whoever broke into the place, had obviously consumed. But there was also a shotgun locked up in a cabinet that was now missing. Tools from inside were used to break the lock and the shotgun was removed along with only one-shot gun shell from the previously full box. The shotgun was a very simple break action one that only held one shell at a time. After each shot was fired, it needed to be opened up, and when this action was done, the spent shot gun shell would automatically eject to the ground. Then you slid a new shell inside and closed the action and you were ready for the next shot. It was not a fast way to reload, but it was a time-proven, and highly reliable shotgun.

Steven asked the name of this man he was talking to and he stated that his name is 'Edward Scott', but he said that Steven should call him 'Ed'. He then went on to explain that there was even a note left behind that apologized that this person who did this didn't have enough money to pay for all the damage she had done to get into the cabin, but with the note was thirty dollars to pay for a new lock for the shotgun cabinet, one shotgun shell, and the food that she had consumed while there. Ed had even laughed that he had never heard of a criminal breaking into the cabin who took the time to wash all the dishes she used as well as some general cleaning up.

"Mr. Scott, how do you know the break in was done by a woman?" Asked Steven.

"Please, call me Ed. Have a look at the handwriting on the note, looks feminine to me" replied Ed. "And I am not trying to sound sexist here, but who else would wash the dishes they used for the cabin owner after breaking in their front door?"

Mr. Scott stated that he had no ill-feelings against whomever did this. Obviously, when they left money to partially pay for the damages and consumed items, there was clearly no intent to be a common criminal even though it was a criminal act. It was also very apparent to Steven that Mr. Scott was a kind man who literally saw the desperation in whomever had done this to his cabin. Steven couldn't help but notice that this man was clearly on the level, which created an instant trust between the two. "Don't spend too much time looking for her, I wouldn't press charges as I think she is already going through too much in her life." With that comment, Steven knew that Ed was a kind and caring man who thought about others too.

Steven knew that with a stolen firearm, there may not be a choice. "Technically Ed, this is a theft of a firearm, which is considered a relatively serious crime. So, I am not sure how the crown counsel office would want this handled, but truthfully, I doubt that we will ever even locate the shotgun, but then there are things about this break in that are very unusual, so we never know what will turn up."

After looking at the note and seeing how the perpetrator had take the time to clean up the mess that she had made, Steven had to agree with Ed that it was probable that their intent was never to commit a crime at all. He figured whomever did this must have been very desperate, and he was also certain that this went against this person's own beliefs, values, and upbringing. Why else would they bother to clean up and to leave some money for some of the damage they had done? He also had to agree that based on the handwriting on the note, it was likely a female who had done this. Steven too felt a bit of compassion for the culprit of this action. He kind of laughed to himself as he had never heard of a person breaking in and cleaning up before. Apart from the stolen shotgun, Steven had a hard time even calling this a crime, yet technically that was for Crown Counsel to decide, not him. But this did leave the question of why the shotgun was taken. Was this to commit a further crime likely out of desperation? Perhaps robbery or even a murder?

Steven walked around the back of the cabin where Ed had discovered footprints in the snow the previous day after he saw his cabin broken into. One set of footprints must have been made by the older man earlier when he first discovered the break and enter in the first place. Earlier, Ed had walked around the back of the building around the back and then towards the woods. Ed wisely decided not to follow the prints but to leave it for the police to look at and search. After rounding the corner to the back of the cabin, Mr. Scott pointed just ahead at the other footprints in the snow. Fortunately, the occasional flake falling today did not obscure the tracks and they were easy to see and follow.

Steven needed to follow these footsteps towards the woods as part of a prudent break in investigation. He first noticed that the footwear was much smaller than most men's feet. This supported the belief of both Ed and he, that the perpetrator was most likely a female.

The footprints led off a short distance behind some bushes and trees and it was back there, about one hundred feet from the back of the cabin that Steven made a grisly discovery. There behind some bushes lay a middle-aged lady who had taken a shotgun blast straight to her face. It was a disturbing scene, so Steven kept Ed from coming there. The mystery of the shotgun was solved too. There it was, lying in the snow, a light dusting on top but not enough to hide it, right next to the lady. The snow all around her head looked to be melted a little with what was once the warm blood that had flowed from her face. Due to the winter cold, there was little decay and no smell of death. Steven had heard that a dead body has a smell like nothing you could ever forget, but this person laying there was too cold to smell.

Although it was clear to Steven that this lady was dead, he still attempted to get a pulse, but she was near frozen and was likely long gone. Technically a police officer is not supposed to determine that someone is dead unless there is decapitation, decomposition or a short list of other possible issues. This was a near decapitation probably due to the shot gun blast, so Steven was certain he could make that decision. Also looking at the amount of blood, there was probably too much lost to maintain life. But he also knew that this was the first violent scene he has ever come across, so gauging the blood loss was something he had no experience in yet.

Being the first death crime, he has ever seen, Steven felt a touch of nausea which he successfully pretended it wasn't affecting him. But deep down he was disturbed to see this lady in the snow like this. There was a feeling of sadness despite not knowing who she is. If she was a victim of a murder, why did she have to die? But he felt it was more likely that she was a victim of suicide, so he wondered what would cause her to want to take her own life in such a violent manor.

Steven went back to his car with Ed and sat him in the front seat to keep him warm while he told him of his discovery. Clearly Ed was quite upset to learn about this death. Steven then contacted the dispatcher through the computer to send more members including the homicide member and the identification member, of course he would also need the coroner to attend, but that was possibly a few hours later. Once

Steven knew that the other officers were confirmed to be on their way, Steven began filling out his report on the computer in his vehicle. While doing the report, he was also trying to simultaneously carry on a conversation with Ed. He learned that Ed was a retired aviation employee who lives down in Surrey British Columbia. Ed owns this cabin and loves to spend July and August staying there with his wife. But sometimes throughout the year he likes to come up for a few days to ensure that it is in good repair. This time he was going to stay for nearly two weeks, but he never anticipated the front door to be broken when he arrived. Steven assured him that the door jam was easily repairable, but Ed replied that he did not have any tools available with him on this trip.

Steven thought about this for a couple minutes before he said anything to Ed, but he offered that on this coming Saturday he could come back on his day off with some tools to get his cabin repaired. He knew that he would have no problem finding one of his new friends or two to come up with him to assist him in not only repairing the door and the door jam, but also with some other simple repairs, up keeps and tasks around the cabin. Ed was very happy to hear that Steven would come that far to assist him on his day off. But Steven told him that it is simply just the brotherly thing for him to do. Ed understood immediately and was very happy to meet Steven.

Unknown to Steven at the time, the dispatcher had also sent an ambulance that turned out to be the first vehicle to arrive on location, but they didn't stay there very long at all. They said that even if the body was warm, she would be dead based on the amount of blood loss and the extent of the injuries sustained to the body. So, the ambulance left after spending a few minutes talking to Steven. This was only a short time after they arrived at the cabin as they really were not needed there.

Steven was returning to his police car, where Ed was still sitting, and as Steven was a good judge of character, he could clearly see that Ed was a kind-hearted man. He could also see that Ed was very upset that his personal shotgun was used to kill this middle-aged lady. This worried Steven as he already came to like Ed despite only meeting him less than an hour before.

Once Steven was seated back in the police car, Ed suddenly asked him, "was this a suicide?'

Steven wasn't sure at first how to respond, fearing that anything he said might upset Ed, but finally he said to him; "that is for the homicide team to determine today, but my best guess is that it will be determined that it was," replied Steven. "but the ultimate decision on that would come from the medical examiner's report which usually takes a few more days. Also, if there is a need for toxicology report, it could take much longer still."

"I should never have left the shotgun here at the cabin," replied Ed, clearly feeling some unjustified responsibility.

Steven could see that Ed was feeling terrible for what had happened. He discreetly typed out a message asking dispatch if there was a victim services volunteer available to attend at the scene. But a short time later the reply came that there was not.

"Ed, I have to tell you, please do not think you are responsible for this. Your shotgun was properly stored and in a locked building. Your ammunition was stored separately in a cupboard in another room. She had to not only break into your cabin, but later she then had to break the lock to the cabinet to get to it to retrieve your shotgun. She also had to look to find the ammunition as they were not stored together. If it was not your shotgun that she used, it would have been someone else's or she would have killed herself in a different way. It could have just as easily been a coil of rope you likely have inside your cabin. Please Ed, you are not responsible for this in the slightest way. She made the choice to do what she did, not you."

Ed was silent a moment before responding; "likely she found the ammunition first. Probably when looking at my various cans of food. Once she found the ammunition, she then searched for the shotgun."

Steven thought about that and had to agree with Ed, that this was the likely sequence of events, not that it really mattered at this point.

Now Steven was feeling even worse for Ed. It was clear to Steven that there is more than one victim for the death of this lady. Likely she left behind friends and family who cared deeply for her too.

During the time they waited for the other officers to show up, Steven had the opportunity to talk more with Ed and learn things about him. Steven was surprised that someone who is staying in this remote location was so community minded. He was very active in fundraising for children's hospitals and medical equipment for children down in the greater Vancouver area as well as children's hospitals and medical equipment throughout North America. Steven couldn't help but think that this seemed very fitting as Ed had both the beard and the personality that made him resemble Santa Claus.

As the two of them were keeping warm in the police car for some time, they engaged in a long conversation where Steven really got to know more about Ed, and he really liked him. During this time, Steven learned that Ed was planning on staying for a couple of weeks at the cabin, and Steven wasn't sure when the homicide and identification sections would be finished with his cabin and would Ed even be able to stay there this evening. Steven once again had assured him that he was able to do the repairs that were necessary to re-secure the front door, but not for a few more days as his first day off would be coming up on this Saturday. But Ed assured him that he had no plans to go anywhere therefore it was not an issue to him that the door would be insecure for a few more days. He brought food with him and had no need to leave the cabin. Besides, how long was his cabin insecure before he arrived? This was a good point that Ed made.

Steven then told Ed that he had some good friends he referred to as their 'brothers' that could show up with him to assist in the repairs and clean up for Ed. Steven could see that Ed was happy to hear that he would have some assistance in the repairs, but still, there was the sadness of the events that had occurred at his cabin. Even telling Ed twice that he had nothing to do with her death, Steven could still see that he was still quite upset about it. Steven made a mental note that on Saturday he would bring by some hot meals for all of them to enjoy and he would leave some leftovers for Ed to have once they left.

It was now about one hour since Steven advised dispatch of the requirement for more members and shortly thereafter the next vehicle showed up at the cabin. This one was the identification officer named Tom who proceeded to photograph everything as well as draw a floor layout and draw a detailed map of the area including the cabin and where the lady's body was discovered. His work was just beginning when the homicide detective arrived on the scene. It didn't take very long for the lone homicide officer to determine that it was almost certainly a suicide. So, the homicide officer made the decision to call the BC Coroner Service to come and retrieve her body from out back. Shortly after that call was made, the homicide officer left to drive back to Prince George.

As the last part of their work, the identification officer, Tom, took one of the food tins that was laying in the garbage bin, to compare the fingerprints to the lady. This was more out of due diligence as they were all but positive that it will be her prints on the empty food can. With Ident having taken the measurements and fingerprint samples and photographs, there wasn't much left for Homicide to do. And this officer was certain that it was just a suicide and nothing more, so he too left the scene.

The next thing the identification officer Tom, would need to do was determine who this lady is and once that identification is positively verified, someone would need to do the notification of her next of kin. Unfortunately, there was no driver's license with her or any other identification that could assist the ident officer with this task. However, he did find car keys in a jacket pocket. The keys were for a Chevrolet vehicle. The identification member told Steven that he will look around the area for Chevrolet vehicles while Steven is waiting for the coroner to arrive. So, Tom decided he would drive around for a few minutes to search for the vehicle the victim arrived in. It was too far away to come by other means, but she could have hitch hiked there. It was a long drive back to Prince George, so why not look around the area first.

Steven was still sitting in his patrol car with Ed in the passenger seat to keep them warm when about half an hour later Tom came back to them outside of the cabin. Steven got out of his car and approached the other officer, Ed followed close behind.

"Hey Steven, I saw a blue Chevrolet Cobalt about half a kilometer away. I clicked the remote and its light blinked. Inside the trunk, I found a lady's purse, so I opened the doors and it retrieved the insurance papers with the address.

"I think I can explain why she broke into this cabin too. When I discovered her car, I noticed that she had taped a vacuum cleaner hose to her exhaust pipe and ran it into the car window. She attempted to poison herself with carbon monoxide gas. But she ran out of gas before she could die. So, my guess is that she then searched for another way to kill herself when she broke into the cabin."

"That is so tragic, she must have felt so down with life."

"Steven, try not to over think why someone would do that, you will drive yourself nuts."

"You are probably correct on that."

"I also looked in the purse and found a driver's license. The description of her height and weight seemed like it could be her, but I wanted to look at her again to compare them. Also, I am going to take her fingerprints before the coroner comes. I hope she has fingerprints on file. I will compare them to the prints on the food tin. Oh, one other thing. There was no money at all in her purse. I mean not one cent. That seemed a little unusual to me."

"Thanks Tom, you saved me from needing to search for her car later. Who knows how long I will be waiting here before the coroner shows up and Mr. Scott is free to return inside his cabin?"

"No problem Steven. I contacted dispatch through the computer and requested a tow truck to take the car away too. I am thinking it is likely hers and if not, it has no business being where it is. It isn't listed as stolen anyway. As soon as I get her prints, I will know. I am going to head back to Prince George and see if I can find some fingerprints of hers in our database." Advised Tom. "Oh, and I am finished with all the photographs and measurements, so Mr. Scott, you are welcome to go back into your cabin."

"Thank you, officer, I really appreciate that." Replied Ed.

It wasn't too long after that when the 'British Columbia Coroner Service's' non-descript black van pulled up in front of Ed's cabin. When it arrived, Steven left the RCMP car, and the preliminary report he was almost finished writing, to meet with them. There was only one occupant in the van, so Steven led him out back and showed him where the body was, and with that and the fact that ident had already taken photographs, Steven was cleared to pick up the shotgun and after ensuring it was made safe and unloaded, he walked back to his car with the shotgun in hand.

At this point, Ed advised him from the porch or entranceway to his cabin, that he never wanted to see that shotgun again, so after the investigation was over, the shotgun would likely be destroyed. Meanwhile, it was placed in the trunk of the police car for transport back to the station in Prince George.

Steven returned out back to assist the coroner's assistant in lifting the body onto the stretcher. The coroner assistant had already placed the deceased into a brown canvas body bag and Steven wondered how he had done that on his own but lifting her onto the stretcher and carrying the corpse to the van was certainly easier using two people.

About half an hour later, Steven was finally cleared to drive back to the station that was located nearly an hour away due to these road conditions. However, before he left Summit Lake, he ensured that Ed would be alright in the cabin and he once again advised him that he would return on his day off with a couple of friends to assist in doing some needed repairs for his new friend Ed. Ed told him that he would be spending his time at the cabin, so there was no hurry in getting the repairs done.

With Steven now being satisfied that Ed would be fine for a few days alone in his cabin, he left to go back to the police station. During the drive back to Prince George Steven did pull over one vehicle for driving too fast for the road conditions. Even as this driver tried to pull over to the shoulder, he was sliding all over the road. A few minutes later, Steven was back on his way.

Once he was back at the station, the shotgun was removed from the trunk of his patrol car and brought inside to be secured in the exhibits lock up. Then Steven went to find Tom the identification officer. He was in his office looking through his magnifier at fingerprints on his worktable in the identification office. Steven wondered if this was for his case, but he doubted it just due to this section's workload.

Steven walked in and asked, "Hi Tom, did you have any luck with the fingerprints you took earlier?"

"Yes, when I got back to the station and investigated the name that I had from the driver's license and insurance papers, I think I know who it is. The prints of the deceased, the ones on the food tin as well as the ones I found on the driver's license all matched. So, I am concluding the identification of this deceased lady. Her name is Janet Boyd, she was fifty-one years old. What did you do with the shotgun? Originally, I thought I should leave it for the medical examiner's office, but after I left, I thought it wasn't needed by them. We already had the photographs and homicide had already left. So, I owe you an apology for leaving that for you to deal with when I should have taken it with me."

"No problem, I took it and I just locked it up in Exhibits."

"Great, I should have taken it for gunshot residue testing, although that seems kind of pointless really, especially now."

"I understand. It has been a long day for me up at Summit Lake. I am going to call it a day and head home. See you in the morning, Tom."

With all that he could complete this day now done, Steven booked off from his day shift and left the station to head back to his home. He was very hungry as he had gone the whole day eating only the muffin and extra-large coffee. Ed did put on the coffee for them, but Steven still had not eaten for several hours.

Once he arrived back at his apartment, he placed a frozen pizza in the oven while he called some friends of his to tell them about Ed and his cabin that needed some repairs. He asked for volunteers to come and assist in patching up his cabin. Although the only damage done from the break-in was to the door frame, and the inside cabinet, there was also some general repairs and fixes that the cabin really needed. Steven explained to these friends that this older man did so much work for fundraising for sick and injured children as a volunteer and that he too was on the level with them. With only a few phone calls, Steven rounded up his group of friends who called themselves the 'brothers' to go out there in a few more days.

Knowing that he now had a small group of guys ready to lend a hand to a nice older man, Steven then went on to remove the pizza from the oven and have a late dinner while watching the evening news on television.

After his dinner was completed, and his cleanup was done, he began putting together a short checklist of items that he thought he would need to bring with him for when he goes back to see Ed with his friends in a few days. He was very impressed that he could round up some friends that he only met about one month ago. But they were a very welcoming group.

The list he put together included some 2 x 4 boards to repair the door jam, along with nails, screws, a new striker plate for the lock, and the various tools to get the work done. He had asked if anyone in the group had some gray paint in tins from a previous home repair to spare him the cost of getting a new tin. He asked for a darker grey to match the door frame and trim of the cabin. But he knew it would be unlikely to find a good match. Of course, given the age of the cabin, he doubted that Ed would care if the color wasn't a perfect fit. It was more important to protect the wood than it was to maintain the aesthetics of the cabin.

After compiling a list of all the materials and tools, Steven sat back and relaxed while he was watching some sitcom on the television before he headed off to bed prior to his next day's shift that would start early the next morning.

After his evening ablutions were completed, he headed off to bed, but the thoughts of Janet Boyd, and what had happened to her to cause her to do what she did, weighed heavily on his mind. He knew he could not sleep right way, so he turned the light back on and read for awhile in an attempt to get sleepier. Finally, about half an hour later he felt that he could fall asleep, and fortunately shortly after, he did.

Chapter Two

The following morning Steven woke up early and got out of bed about one and a half hours before the start of his upcoming day shift. Not long after that, he was consuming his first cup of hot coffee that he made just before he left for the station ready to commence that day's work. He arrived at the police station at his normal time and changed into his uniform before going to talk to Tom from the identification section to find out if there is any new information available for him to consider. Tom would not be in for awhile, so Steven decided to go do the pre-trip inspection on his police car before returning to speak to Tom. Tom did not work the same rotation as patrol constables, he did his time in that work and now spent his career doing the identification work that he enjoyed much more. He was due into the office at eight in the morning.

Once the pre-trip inspection was concluded, he decided to go out on the road for a short time as Tom was still not in the office yet. He managed to get out and write one traffic ticket before returning to the office to see Tom, albeit a bit early for the start of Tom's shift.

"Good morning Tom. I didn't expect to see you here this soon. A little early for you isn't it?"

"Sometimes I don't think I ever leave this place," joked Tom.

"So, what is the good news? Did we get a positive identification on the deceased lady yet?"

"Yes Steven, I ascertained the deceased lady's name yesterday, but it was late before I was certain enough for a notification. Unfortunately, the next of kin have not yet been notified. I thought I would leave that for you." With this last bit of information, Tom was trying to tease Steven.

"I guess that is something I will be doing today. It will be my first time," replied Steven, now a little uncertain about how to approach this terrible part of his job. "No time like now to be the first one for me."

"Good luck with that. I did find out that she has a sister, her name is Marylin Jenkins." Tom now handed Steven a printout with her name and address, along with other pertinent information on it. In addition, there was the date of birth and many other details listed for Janet Boyd. Steven learned from both Tom and via the police computer network called PIRS (Police Information Retrieval System) that there was already a missing person report that Marylin had filed about two days before Steven found her body in the snow behind the cabin. It was a good thing Marylin Jenkins filed this police report or it may have taken much longer to determine who the next of kin is, especially due to the different last name.

Up until the positive identification was done, police avoided notification. Of course, there are times that family members are needed to identify the deceased. But in this particular case, there was pretty much nothing on her face or even dental records that would confirm who she was. This must have been why the notification of her death had not yet been done, they needed the results of the fingerprints. Now the notification would become Steven's job, and he would need to do this during the first half of his shift in case Marylin left for work early. Of course, she could work any hours and Steven wouldn't know that, but he was going with what he thought was the most probable scenario. He was a little uncomfortable as this would be his first death notification. And he had no idea how Marylin would accept the news of her sister's untimely death. But he knew this had to be done and he wanted to get it out of the way as soon as he reasonably could.

With this new information about the victim in his hands, He went to his supervisor to tell him what he would be doing once he left again this morning. Steven left the police station and proceeded to travel to the address of the person listed as Mrs. Boyd's sister, Marylin Jenkins.

Steven was not looking forward to providing the notification of Janet's death. That would be Stevens first task this morning. Steven was uncomfortable doing this duty, but he also knew he would likely have to do this more than once in his policing career. Even the best career for him would have its drawbacks, and Steven already knew this would be one of them. The sister's address was close by to where her deceased sibling lived so, hopefully, Marylin would have a key to that house so Steven could have a look in her residence when he was out that way. He was curious to learn why she would take her own life even though he knew it wouldn't change anything. But Steven was the type of person who liked answers, and just as important, he liked to be able to provide them to others as well.

Steven drove to the address provided to him by Tom and parked his police car out front. He went and knocked on the door. It only took a moment before a lady answered. He introduced himself and he asked her if she was Marylin Jenkins. She replied that she was. He asked if he could come inside for a moment. It was cold in Prince George this time of the year, and he also wanted her to be sitting down when he broke the news to her. Marylin wasted no time inviting him inside and the two sat down in her living room.

He then asked her if she had a sister named Janet Boyd. He could see the instant look of worry on her face. She replied that she does. Steven could see that she wanted to hear the news without delay. He sensed that Marylin had already concluded the worst. Likely she had already determined this long before Steven even showed up this morning.

Once seated in her home Steven began to tell her; "I am so sorry to have to tell you this, but your sister has passed away." Steven felt that the expression 'passed away' would come across better than saying she is dead or that she has died.

"Oh my God, I feared that. But now hearing this news, I am stunned. I have to ask, was her death determined to be a suicide?" Marylin asked. He could see the tears now forming in her eyes as she reached for a nearby box of tissues.

"The identification section said they thought it was, but the coroner and medical examiner have not yet released their findings. They of course provide the official cause of death. But I suspect that is what they will determine." Replied Steven, trying to sound as compassionate as possible. In fact, it was the homicide section and not the identification officer, who stated that they felt it was suicide. Steven said identification instead so that she didn't think of murder as her first thought. He had never done a death notification before this one, and he was told that no matter how many you do, it never gets any easier. He thought back on his training about how to show compassion and at the same time professional boundaries. He was beginning to believe that this was as hard as his instructors told him it would be. He recalled from his training that he should never use the word homicide until it was confirmed, and the investigators said it was okay to release that information. So, although it was the homicide section dealing with that part, he did say the identification section to reduce any undue worry and stress for Marylin.

"I knew my sister was depressed, but I had no idea it was ever this bad. poor girl, she must have felt so much despair."

"How long had she been depressed?" asked Steven. He really wanted to get an impression of who this lady was, and even more important to his curiosity, what had led her to end her life in such a grizzly fashion, despite knowing that getting these answers would never change anything.

"I am not sure. I started noticing that she was behaving differently about six or eight months ago, but it was really just in the last couple of months that I saw a real deep sadness and despair overtake her and that she had withdrawn from all of her friends and even from myself. I tried so hard to reach out to her, tried to get her to tell me what was going on. But no matter what I said or asked, she was reluctant to tell me anything."

"Do you happen to know if she was under the care of a physician, psychiatrist, or a counselor for depression or anxiety or any other issues that you are aware of?" Steven asked this more out of curiosity to learn about Janet, as it really didn't make any difference for the report itself.

"Yes, she was. But that was quite some time ago. Right after her husband left her. She was seeing her family doctor first, but he did refer her to a specialist, I am not sure if it was a psychiatrist or some other professional. But that was about five years ago now. Then about one year ago she seems to spring back with a renewed happiness."

"Did she have a bad marriage back before her husband left her?"

"No nothing like that at all. Sorry, that was a poor choice of my words. Janet was a widow. She had a very good and loving marriage. Her husband Geoff died about five years ago in an industrial accident at the mill he was employed at. He had a decent life insurance policy that he purchased on his own, plus there was the insurance her husband's company left for her. She also would have had his pension that would start when her husband would have turned fifty-five. He had almost twenty-three years with his employer before the accident too. But even though she was well taken care of financially, she was a lonely lady and looking for a loving partner to attempt to replace the void that her deceased husband left for her when he tragically and unexpectedly died."

"I am so sorry to hear all of that." Replied Steven; "I would love to learn more about her. I am curious to know what occurred to lead her in the downward spiral she was likely in."

"Geoff and Janet never had any children. That was really the only sadness in their otherwise very happy life, they both really wanted to have kids. They tried for so long, finally they just came to the realization that it was never to be. Some friends recommended adoption, but before that could happen, Geoff was tragically killed at work. You might have remembered that in the local news here about five years ago?"

"Actually, I have only been in Prince George for a few weeks now. I am still trying to get the street names in my mind." Replied Steven

"I understand. So anyway, Janet, she was completely alone after he died. We all knew she was so lonely. We tried to get her to go out and do things, but she wanted to stay at home alone all the time. I think this was not good for her and it continued for some time. Then a few months ago she thought she found a good man online, but she wouldn't listen to me or any of her friends when we told her that he was just after her money."

"Please tell me what happened to your sister?"

"Oh, from what Janet told me, this man was a very charming person who was out saving the world from Taliban insurgents. This guy told Janet everything she wanted to hear in order to win her over and steal her heart. He had a very good story to tell her about his heroism and being such an amazing patriot for his country. He claimed to be a decorated soldier, a Major in the United States Army. Apparently, he is currently stationed somewhere in the middle east. Over time I learned that she was sending him her money. I told her that she shouldn't do that, and I think he was just scamming her for all the money he could get from her. In fact, am certain of that. I tried to warn her, but she thought she knew better. She trusted him completely and she was certain that his love for her was real. From what she had told me, I could see that he certainly had a silver tongue, but unfortunately no heart of gold to match. I doubt he really was a soldier too, but I have no proof of that. And the only thing he loved was her money."

"How much money are we talking about?" asked Steven.

"It must be about one hundred thousand dollars, but I actually have no idea." Replied Marylin. "She never did want to tell me the total figure. I am certain that in the last few weeks that she had felt extreme shame for being taken by this jerk."

"That is so horrible. I am so sorry to hear about what she has gone through. I have another question for you, would you happen to have access to her home?"

"Yes, I do."

"If possible, I would like to go there and see if I can find any clues as to why she took her life. Certainly, what you have told me makes sense, but I want to know if there is more to this. I know the coroner has not ruled the cause yet, but I am going to go on the assumption that she did plan to end her own life. But please understand that no matter what I find out, I doubt it will ever provide any closure to you at all. I would call this more of a professional curiosity on my part. I would love to learn what I can and hopefully someday I can assist someone else in a similar situation before it is too late."

"I have to go to work, but I am happy to give you the key to her home, it is only a short distance away. And if you can find out anything that may help someone else in the future, I know that Janet would have appreciated that so much as well, as would I. So please look around and learn whatever you can from her home."

"Thank you but you should consider taking the day off work. Besides the fact that your mind will not be focused on your job, you likely have things that need to get done now for dealing with your sister. I am sure there are friends and family you will need to notify? Also, do you think you are good to go in to work after hearing this news?"

"You are probably right. Maybe I am not in the best frame of mind to go to work today. I need to get some things done now that I know she passed away. I will tell my boss that I need a couple of days off to notify family and friends as well as plan for a service for her. Let me get you the key."

"Thank you, I can either return it to you later this morning, or tomorrow I am on a night shift, so I can return it to you in the early evening around seven when I am out on the road."

"Actually, I have a second key to her back door, so there is no hurry, bring it by tomorrow evening when you start your shift or whenever works best for you."

"Thank you, are you sure you are okay to notify her friends and the remainder of your family?"

"Yes, I am sure I can pull myself together. I had sort of wondered about this possibility since I first figured out that she went missing. Still, now that I know, I do feel stunned. I will call my work first, then I will start to call her friends and our family. There isn't too much family left though, our parents died a while back.

"Thank you. Here is my card with my number on it. Please don't hesitate to call me if you need me. You can leave a voice message for me on the office number. I will head over to your sisters' home now to see what I can figure out. Oh, and on the back of the card is the file number for your sister's missing person report that you filed and under that is the file number of her death, the two numbers are linked, but in case you need them for any legal reasons."

"Thank you for your help with this officer, I really appreciate it. Also, I hope you find something in her home to answer questions on this."

"My pleasure but remember that nothing I might find will ever bring her back or provide any real closure to you. But still, I will try my best."

With the keys in hand, Steven returned to his car and drove the short distance to Janet's home. He arrived in front of her house only moments later because the sisters lived close by. It looked like a nice house but possibly a bit too large for just one person to live in. But as Marylin told him, Janet's husband had passed away, so at one time it was shared between the two of them, plus they had hoped to create children which sadly for them had never occurred.

Climbing the front stairs to Janet's home, he approached the front door and opened the screen door often used in the summertime to allow fresh air in but keep the mosquitoes and fly's out. Using the key that Marylin provided to him, he entered the house. Inside he noticed immediately that the heat was turned down very low, in fact, Steven wasn't even sure if it was turned on at all. It was far too cold inside for anyone's comfort, he wondered if he could see his own breath inside her place. After testing that theory, he learned he could not. He wondered if she turned the heat off because she knew she was going to go and end her life or was this some sort of long-term cost-saving measure as she barely had two pennies left to rub together? At least that was the impression he had of her after talking to Marylin.

Steven walked from room to room in her house to get a feel of the home. He got the sense based on the decorations that she was into crafts. He could see knitted blankets on the sofa, needlepoint pictures on the walls, as well as other home-made crafts. He thought she had some real talent, yet Steven would be the first to admit he has no idea of the difficulty of these crafts, yet he respected the amount of work these likely required.

Finally, Steven stopped at her computer which was one of the only things in her home that was turned on. Even the bed side clock in the master bedroom was unplugged. He moved her mouse expecting to see a log-in box on the screen. That log in screen popped up right away, just as he anticipated, and Steven thought to himself that this could be hard for him to get into the computer. But right on the bottom of the monitor there was a Post-It-Note attached and he saw the word 'Benjamin1' and typed that in. He could hear the hard drive buzzing as the computer began to log on and come to life. Steven wondered for a moment if the Post-It-Note was left there on purpose. Most likely it was left there for Marylin, Janet's sister to find.

The first thing Steven did on her computer was to bring up her email program and proceeded to read some of them. It was very interesting to see an argument with a man online who was named 'Benjamin' there on the email program. Perhaps the reason she used that name as a password was a clue to him that he needed to look at Benjamin more closely. Steven started with viewing the most recent email which was a nasty reply to one that Janet had sent him claiming she had nothing left and therefore nothing left to live for. His reply to her clearly indicated he had no empathy for her at all and only viewed her as a source for money. This email would be a good piece of evidence to suggest suicide, so using Janet's printer, he made a copy to attach to his report.

While in the email program, Steven decided to search from the oldest emails from Benjamin in order to better establish a timeline for all that occurred. One of the first things that caught his attention was that Benjamin stated; "this is a much better way to communicate than using that website". Steven didn't want to jump to any conclusions, but he did feel that it was most likely a dating website that they moved away from to continue their communications by email. There were literally hundreds of emails between these two people. Although she sent him far more than she received from him. At quick glance, she sent four or even five emails to each one received from him. Steven would need hours or even days to read them all, so he decided to jump ahead a few weeks and see what he could find out. Steven had never heard of the website that he read they were initially using, but to him, it sure sounded like it was for lonely people hoping to find love and a partner.

Reading one of Janet's random emails showed Steven that Benjamin was thanking Janet for assisting him with a loan and he assured her that the military payroll system would be up and running again shortly and he would be able to repay her money as soon as that had occurred. Reading this clearly set off an alarm bell in Steven's mind. Not that the military pay system doesn't have its flaws, but how long could it possibly be down?

Looking through other emails at random Steven began to piece together a preliminary story that Benjamin was telling her. He claimed to be a Major in the United States Army in an infantry unit stationed in Afghanistan manning a forward operating base. That may be real, but Steven thought that this was a convenient story for an internet scammer to use. Then Steven was thinking about how if the military pay was down, the store on base would probably extend credit as it would probably be down for all the soldiers at this base. Also, there would likely be nothing to spend his money on at a forward operating base. Although Steven was not certain, he did believe that they would never have enough staff to warrant having a store. But even if he was back on the main base like Kandahar, Benjamin could still get things he wanted or needed. Now Steven was very suspicious of this so-called soldier, so he read further on in the emails.

In another email just before the one thanking Janet for the money she had sent him, Benjamin was explaining that with the payroll system down, he could not make his mortgage payment back home in Arizona. She asked how much he needed for his mortgage payment. This was sounding a little more reasonable to Steven, but still, he knew that 'Benjamin was nothing short of a con artist and a predator. But any doubts he may have had were removed when he saw Benjamin's reply. It stated he was in arrears and was facing foreclosure from the bank unless he paid $5000 right away. Then he asked if she would send that money via western union to his sister to make the payment as soon as possible. Steven wanted to yell 'no, don't do it' at the computer when he read that she would send it that very day.

Steven was no accountant, nor a mortgage manager at a bank, but he really doubted that a mortgage company would start a foreclosure procedure on only five thousand dollars. The legal fees alone would far exceed the amount that was actually in arrears. It would likely start as a lean against the property. Also, if it was learned by the public that the arrears of the mortgage were caused by a payroll issue while the mortgage holder was fighting for his country overseas, the negative publicity could be overwhelming for that financial institute, especially in the United States where there is high esteem for soldiers fighting for their country. Third, Steven believed that when a soldier is off at war, the military assumes power of attorney on civil matters such as this through the 'Judge Advocate General's office'. In addition, there would likely be some sort of mortgage insurance for just that sort of issue. But it was obvious to Steven that Janet didn't know any of these key pieces of information that would have likely caused her to think twice before sending over her money to a person reported to be his sister.

As Steven continued to visually scan the numerous emails displayed on the screen, he read in another one much later on that the $5000 only took care of the interest on what he owed the bank, and he was once again back in arrears just on the interest alone. Now Benjamin went on to explain that he is actually in the Army National Guard and had to leave his higher paying job back home to go serve his country. That is why he couldn't meet his mortgage payments while on deployment. It was also noted by Steven that Benjamin was a very smooth talker and knew exactly what to say to get Janet to fall in love with him earlier on, pretty much just like her sister Marylin had said he was. But Steven also believed that Benjamin was not a soldier at all, nor was he in Afghanistan, and he most certainly looks nothing like the lone photo he sent to her. Little did he know at this time, how right he actually was. But one thing was certain to Steven, and that was the fact that Benjamin, or whoever he really was, spun a really good story explaining his hardships.

Now that he established that whoever was posing as Benjamin was clearly a con-artist, Steven used his cell phone to call a relatively new friend of his, Jorge, who is a computer expert at a local electronics store. They met shortly after Steven arrived in Prince George, as Steven was new in town, he only knew a handful of people, but he quickly established himself with them.

Speaking to his friend, he was told to open the email in the browser and copy the email transit information and paste it into a specific web site that his friend had him bring up on her computer. It showed that this email had originated from Toronto. This surprised Steven's friend as he was certain it would have come from either Nigeria or possibly Ghana, Ukraine or even Russia.

Steven explained that Benjamin had claimed to be in the US Army, later that was changed to the Army National Guard. It may be a small change to some, but he felt this might be significant in the scheme to get money. His friend asked him if there was a photo of Benjamin on her computer. Steven said there were only a single one that he had located so far.

"Can you email the photo to me?"

"I can be in big trouble for that," replied Steven.

"Don't worry, I will not tell anyone" laughed Jorge.

Although Steven trusted Jorge like a brother, he knew it was wrong to do on a privacy level, but he thought about this for a minute and decided that this could help him to close this file and maybe provide answers for the sister Marylin. So, the ends justified the means in his mind. With that thought, he sent an email to his friend from Janet's email account. Even while they were still on the phone, another email came into Janet's computer. But this one was from his friend Jorge on the phone. It showed the exact same soldier but with a different name than the one he knew of as Benjamin. In this case it was depicted as a soldier who was listed as killed in action only three years before in the Korangal Valley in Afghanistan. The real soldier was displaying the rank of Major, but his name tape was covered up by the gear he was wearing and was therefore unreadable in the picture. The article went on to say his name was Major Klassen. Steven's first thought after seeing this is that at least Benjamin got the Afghanistan part of his story correct. After discovering this on-line photo and article, he printed out the story of this real soldier's tragic death in combat using Janet's printer once again.

Steven's friend on the phone also suggested looking at the bookmarks on the browser for a banking program as there was a good likelihood that the log-in information would automatically fill in. Steven searched and found a bookmark for the Canadian Imperial Bank of Commerce. Clicking on this bookmark opened the browser window and discovered that his friend was correct about the autofill of passwords and usernames. Steven could access it with little difficulty.

With this information, he thanked his friend and disconnected the call to pursue more time on Janet's computer.

It was during the time that Steven was on the banking website that he really noticed something unusual there. He could bring up the accounts based on dates, so he looked at some past statements. Only two years ago Janet had a decent savings account, Registers Retirement Savings Plan, a small mortgage that would be paid off in short order. She was well off and all set up for retirement in about five years without owing anything short of a small mortgage that may likely be paid out by then. Instead, over the past few months, her savings account was drained to empty, and her registered retirement savings plan was completely gone. Also, her home was now re-mortgaged for a larger amount, and worse still, Steven felt she was in serious danger of her getting a foreclosure order on her home due to so many missed payments and not enough income now to match the outgoing.

Armed with this information he locked up the home and left for his patrol car. He figured he was showing on this call far longer than he was entitled to do so, but he never heard from his dispatcher about other calls holding. His portable radio never enquired as to what he was doing. He did notify the dispatcher via the car computer that he was going to do a death notification and then later he stated that he is going to the deceased persons home for a follow up. But now he must return to the station to work on this report.

On the way he had the idea that he should go to the Canadian Imperial Bank of Commerce that Janet was dealing with regarding her mortgage. He entered the branch and asked to speak to the manager. They went into an office, and Steven began to explain what he needed to know. But the bank manager politely advised him that until they get the official notification that Janet Boyd is deceased; they cannot tell him very much if anything. Steven understood this, but still he was disappointed in not learning more from the bank. But he was impressed with the bank for taking their customers' security and privacy seriously. So, Steven left the financial institution to go back to the station. But once on the road, he got yet another idea. If there were foreclosure proceedings against Janet, there would be an open file at the courthouse and that would probably be public record. As it was a civil proceeding, not criminal, it would never show on the RCMP computer system.

Steven entered the courthouse in Prince George. At this courthouse, it was both a provincial and a supreme court in one building. But a foreclosure file does not need to be opened in the nearest courthouse to the property, only in the same province. So even if they didn't hold the file, they would be able to look it up. He went straight to the court registry and looked for the civil counter. Once there he asked the clerk at the counter if there was a foreclosure file or any active lawsuits against the name Janet Boyd. It only took a moment for the clerk to type her name into the computer and advise him that there is, in fact, a relatively recent file. The court used a program called CEIS, which was an acronym that stood for 'Civil Electronic Information System'. It showed a file opened with the style of cause of 'The Canadian Imperial Bank of Commerce vs Janet Boyd'. So, she wrote the file number out on a piece of paper handed it to him and sent Steven to the 'File and Search' counter to have them pull the file for him to physically look at it. Fortunately, these files are considered public, so Steven did not need to have a warrant or even provide a reason to look at it. If it was a family file, he would not have been given access even if he is a police officer and on duty, at least not without proper authorization to view it.

     A couple of minutes later the file was brought out and handed to him right at the counter and Steven opened it to look at the contents. It showed the case as 'The Imperial Bank of Commerce vs Janet Boyd' just like the first lady had said, and the file was only a couple weeks old. Inside the file was the Notice of Claim, and Steven noticed that there was a redemption amount that was likely close to the total value of the home itself that was showing in this document. There was no way she could have paid off that bill in time, if at all. But the next document that caught his attention surprised him even more. It was an 'affidavit of service' that the process server filed this affidavit only the day before Steven found her. Also, looking at the date listed in the body of the affidavit as to when and where she was served, Janet was served with this notice of claim at her house only three days before she was found by Steven. Of course, he still needed the medical examiners' time of death to be certain how long she was there, but with Marylin's evidence, he had it narrowed to within 2 days. Steven wondered if her being served the Notice of Claim was the final straw that broke Janet. Was this simply more than she could take? In Steven's mind, it most certainly was. He felt so badly for her. She had been through so much.

The clerk at the counter asked Steven if he wanted copies of those two documents, and when he said yes, she then left for the photocopier. Steven thanked her for the copies and getting the file for him to view. He then left to go back to the police station with copies of these documents in his hand.

Once inside the station, Steven's sergeant asked him if he made the notifications. Steven replied that he had, and he spoke to the sister about her death. In addition, he also received a possible motive for the suicide. Steven then advised his boss that there may even be a crime here. Not a murder, but probably a fraud that led to her suicide.

They went into an office where the door was closed behind them. At first Steven wondered if he was to be reprimanded for taking so long on this file. But then it became evident; his supervisor didn't want others overhearing him talking because this supervisor likely felt Steven was being overzealous in his work as few police officers this new on the job would discover a crime causing death from a simple suicide. But at least this supervisor was willing to listen to Steven, even if he did seem a touch sceptical to the idea.

Steven told him all about what he had discovered from the computer (omitting the part about his friend looking at the photos). He told him about the mortgage being in arrears, and about a foreclosure file that was opened and how she was served a few days before he found her. And most importantly he told about the apparent romance scam to get her money. Steven was surprised when his sergeant told him that he should consider calling the RCMP Criminal Intelligence Program section in 'E Division', down in the lower mainland to get some advice from them on how to proceed.

Prior to this, he was certain that his Sargent was going to tell him not to bother even looking this far, and that certainly he had other more important things to do like finish off other files or help out by taking some calls. But instead, his Sargent encouraged him to continue looking into this. Perhaps this was simply a good learning experience for a new constable? No matter the reason, Steven was now feeling very good about himself and for the work that he was doing. But at the same time, he was always mindful of the other files he had on the go as well. He couldn't let them sit too long without completion as the numbers of files just get larger. But his Sargent encouraged him to call RCMP Criminal Intelligence Program in the lower mainland for more instructions and information.

So that is exactly what Steven did. He took a seat at a vacant desk and called the RCMP Criminal Intelligence Program section in the Vancouver region at 'E Division' headquarters. He spoke to an officer named Robert. Robert listened to John explain the situation in detail, interrupting only periodically for the occasional clarifying question for him. After Steven finished explaining, Robert then told him that this is something called a 'Romance Scam'. Then Robert provided Steven with a detailed run-down on how it works.

He explained to Steven, "Romance scammers create personal profiles using stolen photographs of attractive people for the purpose of asking others to contact them. This is often known as 'catfishing'. Communications are exchanged between the scammer and victim over a long period of time until the scammer feels they have connected with the victim and gained enough trust to ask them for money."

"Frequently the victims are lonely males or females who are genuinely looking for true love online. And when they believe they have found it; the scammer then makes requests from them. These requests may be for gas money, bus or airplane tickets to visit the victim, it may even be medical or education expenses. There is usually the promise the scammer will one day join the victim in the victim's home. The scam usually ends when the victim realizes they are being scammed or stops sending money altogether. The duration of the scam itself really depends on the vulnerability of the victim. Some may figure it out before any money is lost, others may lose it all. Some studies suggest that the average amount is about five thousand dollars, but this figure is very subjective as very few victims ever report these crimes. They fail to report them for fear of being treated like they are stupid for falling for such a scam in the first place."

Robert continued; "these criminal networks defraud lonely people all around the world with false promises of both love and romance combined with the false belief of a loving long-term relationship. The victims believe they have finally found the one special person for them, their true 'soulmate'. Scammers post profiles on dating websites, social media accounts, classified sites, and even online forums to search for their new victims. The scammer usually attempts to obtain a more private method of communication such as an email or phone number to build trust with the victim as well as to get off the website where they first met. This is because reputable dating websites will seek to remove scammers to maintain their good name. Scammers prey on the victim's false sense of a relationship to lure them into sending money."

Steven asked, "So, in this case, he told her that he was facing foreclosure on his house back in the United States. Is that a common way it is done?"

Robert continued; "There are many ways that they do it, sometimes the scammer may say that their boss has paid them in postal money orders and asks the victim to cash the forged money orders and then wire the money to the scammer. The bank eventually reverts the money order to cash but not the wire transfer, leaving the victim to pay the bank for the bogus money orders. Or the scammer says they require money for flights to the victim's country because they are being held back in their home country by a family member or estranged spouse. In all cases, the scammer never comes, or instead says that they are being held against their will by immigration authorities who are demanding bribes be paid before they can be released. Another common method is that the scammer says they have had gold bars or other valuables of theirs seized by customs and need to pay the taxes on them before they can recover their items and join the victim in their country. And this is just the tip of the iceberg. Would you like me to continue?"

Steven was finding this discussion very interesting and he replied, "If you don't mind and have the time, I certainly would like to hear more about this, I find it very interesting to learn about this."

"Okay, I like that you are interested, I wish more people would be," continued Robert. "The scammer meets the victim on an online dating site. The scammer claims to live in a foreign country, which is often true, but not always. They tell the victim that they fell in love, but then needs money to join the victim in his or her country. Or, the scammer says they are being held against their will for failure to pay a bill or require money for hospital bills. Another way, the scammer says they need the money to pay their phone bills in order to continue communicating with the victim. And then there are the medical reasons, the scammer says they need the money for their own or their parents' urgent medical treatment. And the last of the common ones, the scammer says they need the money to complete their education before they can visit the victim."

"Common ones? You mean there are more?"

"Oh Steven, you have no idea. And when we have thought we heard every romance con job out there, they come up with so many more. Let me tell you the less common ones that still work on some people. The scammer is in fact employed directly or indirectly by a dating website, with a share of the victim's member or usage fees passed on to the scammer to keep them chatting and keep them using their service. Many of these ones originate in Ukraine or Russia. You see they have a pay per use system for chatting. So, the victim meets someone who seems very interested in chatting with them. The purpose is to get them to keep sending the dating site money to continue the conversations. Of course, this person has no desire for a relationship with the person or persons here. In fact, this is a job to them so they may even be married themselves. But the more they can keep the victim chatting through their website, the more money they make. "

Robert continued to explain, "some romance scammers seek out a victim with an obscure fetish or sexual desire and will make the victim think that if they pay for the scammer's plane ticket, they will get to live out their sexual fantasy with this scammer. Still other scammers like to entice victims to perform sexual acts on webcam. They then record their victims and later play back the recorded images or videos to them, and then attempt to extort money in order to prevent them from sending the recordings to friends, family, or employers. The scammers often discover the list from their targets social media sites such as Facebook or Twitter."

"But then there is the more common method like the one you discovered when you first called; this is a rapidly growing technique scammers utilize. They like to impersonate American military personnel deployed overseas. Scammers prefer to use the images, names, and profiles of soldiers as this usually inspires confidence, trust, and admiration in their female victims. Military public relations often post information on soldiers without their families or personnel knowing this, so images are stolen from these websites by organized internet crime gangs often operating out of Nigeria or Ghana. Some pictures come from combat correspondents who are doing a legitimate job, but others take those photos and use them for criminal purposes."

"My friend did tell me it was often from Nigeria or Ghana. But I traced the IP address to Toronto."

"We will talk about Toronto in a few moments but let me continue with this first. These scammers tell their victims they are lonely, or supporting an orphanage with their own money, or needing financial assistance because they cannot access their own money in a combat zone. The money is always sent to a third party to be collected for the scammer. Sometimes the third party is real, sometimes fictitious. Funds sent by Western Union and MoneyGram do not have to be claimed by showing identification if the sender sends money using a secret passphrase and response. The money then can be picked up anywhere in the world. Some scammers may request cryptocurrencies as an alternative payment method. There is very little tracking if any."

"It was one of those very methods that was used to trick Janet," replied Steven. "But why do they allow pickup without identification?"

"Simple, if you go away on vacation and your wallet gets lost or stolen, you will not have identification to use to receive money. If you contact a friend or family to wire you some emergency cash, how would you get it? A password is a good thing that is being used by the scammer to do bad things."

"I understand. It makes sense to me now."

"You had mentioned Toronto a moment ago. Now we will talk about that; There is a notorious group, called the 'Black Axe' cult or simply 'Black Axe'. They have set up business here in Canada. This elusive group is feared in Nigeria for its extreme brutality. They have been exerting undue influence over the Nigerian government for several years now. In Canada, they have been engaging in organized crime and extreme violence, torture and even murder. "

Robert went on to explain the thing that caught the police's attention here in Canada. It was their matching outfits. "They wear high yellow socks and black berets that featured an emblem of manacled hands, and an axe breaking through the chain. There were two men who were each being investigated separately for fraud, one of them was in British Columbia and the other one was in Toronto. But it was their presence together, in identical outfits, that sent Canadian investigators on this new lead". It was this lead that sent the investigators deep into the heart of a Nigerian subculture and the African nation's political hierarchy.

"This turned out to be a Nigerian 'confraternity' now called 'The Black Axe', otherwise known as the

Neo Black Movement of Africa (NBM). This elusive group is feared in Nigeria for its brutality, as I had said, but they are getting established here in Canada too. They are known for engaging in organized crime and violence. Aside from fraud and money laundering, they are believed to be involved in street-level crime but mostly in Toronto. Of course, there is a considerable amount of street-level crime in Nigeria committed by this group;" but Robert was mainly referring to their actions here in Canada. "Everything from intimidation to kidnapping to murder and the large-scale movement of stolen goods on a transnational scale."

"This group is referred to as a 'confraternity'. This is because Sources indicate that the Black Axe is, in fact, a religious cult. The Black Axe confraternity and some other cult groups were formed in the 1980s as tools of the Nigerian military and they in turn formed street cult groups."

"What is a confraternity?" asked Steven.

"Technically it is a brotherhood, especially with a charitable or religious purpose. But in this case, they happen to be their own charity. As I previously told you, some of our sources state that the Black Axe confraternity is also known as the Neo-Black Movement of Africa. However, other sources indicate that, according to the Neo-Black Movement, they are not the Black Axe confraternity nor are they a secret cult. Some say that the Black Axe confraternity is a 'splinter group' of the NBM, or Neo-Black Movement, and indicates that, since 1985, the NBM has worked to dissociate itself from the Black Axe Confraternity's activities. But this remains to be seen and is only speculation at this time."

"I have never heard of this group before I called you today. How do they find their members?"

"That is a great question, Steven. A human right's watch group report indicated that the Black Axe confraternity forcibly recruits new members back in Nigeria. We are not aware of forced recruiting here in Canada yet, but that does not mean it isn't happening, it merely means we have not heard of it happening here up to this point. According to Vanguard, a Lagos-based newspaper, the Edo state Police Public Relations Officer indicated that generally, cult activities are secretive. Information on rituals, oaths of secrecy, and use of symbols or particular signs of the Black Axe confraternity could not be found among the sources consulted by the Research Directorate within the time constraints of this Response."

"Has this group ever been known to be violent?"

"Boy have they ever. They have been known to murder and torture people. They are feared by the authorities and government workers of Nigeria for their cruelty and viciousness. If they ever want to send a message to someone, they usually take a loved one and torture them to death in the most painful of ways imaginable. Fortunately, for the most part, these types of crimes have not occurred in Canada, those are mainly in Nigeria and sometimes in Ghana too. At least that is what we believe. Here in Canada, or should I say in developed nations in North America and Europe, the bulk of their crimes are white collar for the time being. Romance fraud is a huge part of their financial scams, but so is stealing high-end automobiles for shipment back to Africa. Other crimes they are suspected of doing here in Canada include extorsion, fraud, and some robberies, and of course violence. Romance scams are their biggest profit makers, but basically, they are not a nice group of people."

"Robert, I want to thank you for giving me your time and all the information you provided to me. My intent was simply to close a suicide file and try to give a reason to the victim's family for why she did this. You have given me so much more than I could have imagined. I must admit after talking with you today, you have caught my interest and I am going to do some reading on this group as I never heard of them before talking to you today."

"It is my pleasure to assist you, Steven. Please do not hesitate to call me here at E Division with anything I can do for you or if you have any further questions. That is what we are here for," replied Robert.

With all this vast amount of new information Steven just learned, he told his supervisor all about it and the group Black Axe. But Steven was reminded by his supervisor that his job was to close the file as to her suicide. If Steven has found another crime committed, he could certainly pass the information on for further investigation, but he was not a detective, he was a junior officer fresh out of depot training.

Steven knew his hunch was little more than a strong suspicion at this point, so he would have to gather more information before he could pass it on to an organized crime investigation group within the RCMP. As Steven was a general duty constable, he would have to do this when he was not working on his normal caseload. He decided right then that this would be something he wanted to do.

Chapter Three

Steven had just shown up for the last shift of his two nightshifts before his days off. Once he arrived at the police station, he noticed some new papers placed in his mail slot. It was the medical examiner's report from the coroner's office. Just as he and everyone else who dealt with this file suspected, Janet Boyd's' cause of death was determined to be from suicide by shotgun blast to the face and head, followed by excessive loss of blood. What Steven did not know until this report arrived was that the wound itself was actually survivable had she received medical intervention right away. But she had lost too much blood to survive more than a couple of hours without medical assistance. Likely being in the cold also prolonged the suffering for some time too. Steven felt almost sick at learning these new facts about her demise. He could not imagine what the wounds would look like had she been found in time for medical intervention.

Even though Steven never knew Janet, he saw her pictures and she seemed like quite an attractive middle-aged lady. In addition, he learned about how nice a person she was. How she was caring and attentive, and a loving lady who most men would really appreciate. He couldn't help but feel she should have been able to find a good partner locally, why did she need to look online or more importantly look far abroad for love? He knew that these are questions that he would never know the answers to, but he thought about them anyway. Since learning about the scam committed against her, Steven had constantly felt anger towards the perpetrator of this crime. Preying on the weak always made Steven mad. He was the type of person to stand up to bullies at school to defend not only himself, but the smaller kids there too. But maybe that is why he went into law enforcement in the first place. He cared deeply about the underdog. He hated seeing anyone get exploited for anything, and if he could do something about it, he was determined to do just that. This was who Steven really was. It wasn't that he wanted to be someone's hero, it wasn't even that he wanted the satisfaction of knowing he was a good man for himself, it was simply because for him this was the right thing to do.

With all of this information plus the newly arrived coroners report now in his hands, Steven could finally close off this file on her death. Unfortunately, he was still troubled by this. In the back of his mind, he knew that the story was far from being closed. He felt a need and a responsibility to continue investigating what had happened to Janet. He needed to know what had occurred to her that led her to this horrible end.

About one hour after the start of his shift, Steven finally got out on the road. After his daily pre-trip inspection of the police car, he drove immediately to Marylin's home to return Janet's key to her. As he drove up to her home, she had seen him through the window, waved at him and then came to the door before he could even walk up and ring the doorbell.

"Good evening Constable, please come in."

"Thank you. How have you been doing?"

Looking sad, Marylin commented, "all things considered, I guess I am doing okay."

"I have no doubt this has been a very difficult time for you. Once again, I am so sorry for your loss. There are bereavement services available for you if you would like. I should have offered that to you before, but, honestly, you are the first notification I have ever done."

"Thank you, constable, I appreciate that. And I would have never known I was your first. You showed a good amount of compassion and I really appreciated how you broke the news to me."

"I am here to return the key to you, and I wanted to tell you personally about the coroners' findings as well as what I have learned."

"Okay, please tell me?"

"Well, as I had suggested to you before, it was in fact ruled as a suicide. I am not surprised at all. I have learned some things though. She gave her on-line boyfriend a considerable amount of money."

"I figured that. Was it more than the one hundred thousand dollars like I guessed?"

"Sadly, it was much more;" replied Steven

"Oh my God!" Clearly Marylin was shocked to hear this information. "I am not sure I really want to know, but please do tell me how much money we are talking about?"

"Actually, I have no real idea yet. I looked at your sister's computer and saw a lot of money transfers to him. I would need to spend some time looking through every single email and add them all up. But what I do know for sure is she had cashed out all her registered retirement savings plan, and that money is long gone. She remortgaged the home to the highest amount she could, and that money is also gone. I also found that the Canadian Imperial Bank of Commerce had opened a foreclosure file with the Supreme Court of British Columbia. So, in a few more months she would have been homeless too. And with all the money spent, she would have been both homeless and penniless too. The only thing she would have had was her husband's pension of which I think would only afford her a cheaper rental location. Probably a dump too."

"I am absolutely stunned to learn this. I had no idea it was that much money." Clearly Marylin was sad to hear this. "She had so much going for her. Her husband worked so hard to ensure that they would be comfortable in their retirement. When he died, he had life insurance that was to take care of her as well. And then this jerk shows up and ruins everything."

"Likely it was far more than one jerk; these are probably organized jerks who are working together. But I do not know that for certain."

"Can you find out?"

"It wouldn't be easy. But I do want to learn more about this particular group that I suspect is behind your sister's theft."

"Please Steven, is there anything at all that I can do to assist you in determining this?" asked Marylin.

"Actually, there is. This is a little unethical of me to ask this, but under the circumstances, I think it would be okay." Replied Steven.

"Please tell me."

"Well, I am not a detective, I am a relatively new constable fresh out of depot training in Regina. But what I would like to do is this; on my own time, I want to learn whatever I can about a criminal group that does these types of crime. It is likely that this is the same group that targeted your sister, but at this time I have no evidence of this, it is just a guess based on the way the money was taken from her. So, what I would like to do with your permission is borrow your sisters' computer for possibly a few months to really read and study all the emails thoroughly, as well as try to track down where the money has gone. You need to know that I will not be able to retrieve the money from these thieves, but I do want to find out where it went. What the unethical part I am asking is in taking your sisters computer to do this at my home and not on police time at the station."

"Well, I have a copy of her latest will and earlier today I carefully reviewed it, and technically the computer is now mine. So, I am happy to loan it to you. Take your time, even if it takes you one year, that is fine with me too. But can you call me periodically to tell me what you are learning about her case?"

"Of course. And thank you. But it is essential that you understand there is likely nothing I can do to retrieve your sisters' money. Nor am I likely to be able to provide any real closure to you. My hope is to be able to assist someone in the future from going through a situation like Janet did." With that said, Steven knew that if he learned anything that would be considered contentious in a criminal investigation, he would not be able to pass that information on to her like he said he would, but he knew she would understand that.

Marylin nodded that she understood the limits on what Constable Browne could and could not do, but also, she stated that it is important for the memory of Janet to attempt to help others from falling victim too. She then suggested that Steven come by her sisters' home after work the following morning and Marylin would be there for him to collect the computer.

The remainder of his shift proved to be very routine. There was one domestic disturbance, and a late-night noise complaint. Other than that, there was not too much happening in the area of Prince George that Steven patrolled. So, at the end of his shift at six the following morning he booked off and went to Janet's house to meet Marylin there. She let him inside the home where he disconnected the computer and took it to his car. At first he thought of leaving the keyboard, monitor, mouse and all other items there as he only needed the main body of the computer, but thought he should bring it all so that he could search on the internet on his own computer while examining the contents of Janet's computer. Once it was secured in his car, he re-entered Janet's house and talked some more with Marylin.

"Do you have a funeral service planned for Janet yet?"

"I was going to talk to you about that. We are having a memorial service later today in the late afternoon or more like the early evening, it will be at 5:30." She replied. "I am not sure how I am going to pay for it. Her estate is likely pretty much worthless now. But fortunately, the funeral home has a deferred payment plan. I am certain they have dealt with situations like this before."

"I can only imagine. I will try to attend, but I am just coming off the night shift, so I am very tired. But I would like to attend and to be there if it is alright with you?"

"Thank you, Constable, that is very kind of you, please don't feel obligated, but you are certainly welcome to come."

"Please, call me Steven. Actually Marylin, there is one other thing I was wondering if I could get from you. Would it be possible to get Janet's banking statements when you are done with them, or supply me with photocopies? That may provide a lead for me to learn the direction of the money that left her."

"Of course, you can have copies of those. I will photocopy them for you as I need these for myself too. So, I will do that for you sometime this weekend. Can I put them in an envelope with your name on it and take it to the police station?"

"That would be perfect; or call me and I can come pick them up. Whatever is easiest for you. Thank you. And I hope I will be able to attend the service and see you later this evening." With that, Steven left to go home and get some much-needed sleep.

He arrived home only a few minutes later. Knowing that he would like to attend both the service, and a dinner with some friends of his after the memorial service, Steven had gone straight to bed, and it wasn't long before he was sound asleep from a long night at work.

Steven woke up a few hours later and decided he received enough sleep to attend the memorial service for Janet. So, he shaved and showered, then he put on a nice suit before heading out the door to attend the funeral of a lady he had never actually met before. But he was attending this not just for the memory of Janet, but also for Marylin too.

Steven had arrived at the memorial service about ten minutes before it was scheduled to start. Upon entering the funeral chapel, he was spotted immediately by Marylin. She came right up to him and gave him a friendly hug; "Thank you for coming, I know Janet would have really appreciated you being here. I can say that I certainly do appreciate it too."

"Thank you Marylin. Of course, I am so sorry we have to meet under these unfortunate circumstances."

"I am too. Please take a seat anywhere you like and there will be beverages and snacks to follow right after the service."

"Again, thank you for your invitation." With that said, Steven took a seat halfway between the font and the back of the chapel. The service was not scheduled to be very long, and there were many empty seats, but it was a large funeral chapel and there were still plenty of people in attendance. The service was very touching, and it painted a nice picture of who Janet really was. Steven almost felt like he knew her before the funeral, and this service only compounded that feeling of familiarity he had with her. At the front of the chapel was a large photograph of Janet. It was obviously taken at much happier times.

Janet was clearly loved by all of those who knew her, it was obvious to Steven that she will be missed by each and every one of them. Besides her immediate family in attendance, she also had a few friends there to say their final goodbye's, along with them were some neighbors. Steven guessed that some of the people in attendance were her deceased husbands' co-workers, and Steven even spotted the bank manager from the CIBC when she waved hello to Steven from her seat, clearly recognizing him despite the fact that he was not in his police uniform that evening.

Even the chaplain commented about how Janet will be dearly missed and that she was appreciated by so many. Although Steven thought to himself that the minister likely always said that, he believed it was probably true in Janet's case. He also went on to say that she is in a happier place now that she has been reunited with her husband in Heaven.

While seated in a pew at the funeral chapel, Steven noticed one person who came in late, about halfway through the service. He seemed out of place to Steven. Perhaps it was due to Steven's recent conversation with Robert, the RCMP Criminal Intelligence Program officer from E Division down in the lower mainland. This person was a black man who walked in during the second half of the service. He seemed more interested in getting the services leaflet and looking at all the people in attendance than he did listening to the service being conducted by the chaplain. There was almost an uncomfortableness about this man. He didn't look nervous, but he sure didn't seem at ease either. Steven would never have noticed this person if he was simply just another black man in a crown. What caught Steven's attention was the fact that he looked to be someone who was from Nigeria, not that Steven had much experience observing people from Nigeria but he new that this person didn't seem North American either. Also, there was the fact that he seemed to study everyone in attendance at the funeral, even if it was only for a second or two for each one. It was like he was trying to remember the faces of everyone who was present. Steven wondered to himself what was this man's purpose here, what was his story, what was he trying to learn from this funeral service? And more important, was he really a friend or true acquaintance of Janet, or was he here for some other purpose yet to be determined?

Maybe Steven was just being too suspicious after learning about Black Axe? Or maybe his instincts as a police officer were starting to seriously develop. Regardless of the cause of alerting Steven, the moment the service was over, this man moved quickly to the door and left the funeral service like he was in a big hurry. Steven wanted to stay for a short while but decided to follow this man outside and see if he could get the license plate number of his vehicle or some other information to help identify him.

Unfortunately, even though Steven was less than a minute behind him, when he exited the chapel out onto the street, Steven could not see him anywhere. Coincidently there was also a bus just leaving the bus stop right out in front and there were also some cars on the road. Steven was not able to quickly scan the bus to see if he could spot this man on board, nor did he have enough time to also look into the cars that were leaving the area at that exact same time. So, this man simply disappeared into the streets of Prince George in the early evening darkness. Disappointment entered his mind, but he knew that these things happened.

At first, Steven thought that maybe he was merely being too suspicious of this man. After all, Janet could have had many friends from several different races and cultures. Steven took pride in knowing he didn't have a racist bone in his body, but that alarm bell going off in his head was very strong, and he was rapidly learning to put his trust in it. Also, the nagging feeling that Janet was in fact a victim of the Black Axe group would not leave his mind. He couldn't help but feel that this was the group that targeted her.

Steven, realizing that he would not find this man, had re-entered the funeral chapel. Marylin came up to him and said, "I thought you left without saying goodbye."

"No, nothing like that. I just thought I recognized someone," Steven replied to her. Although this was not true, Steven didn't want to have Marylin concerned for what might be absolutely nothing at all.

"Well, come over to the foyer as we are about to serve beverages and snacks."

"Thank you, I would love to."

Steven attended the foyer and although he didn't consume any of the snacks, he did get a cup of coffee for himself. Coming off the night shift and then sleeping all day, he was still a little tired and this was sort of like a morning coffee to him. Also, he wanted to wake up some more before his dinner meeting with some new friends he met since relocating to Prince George. He took the opportunity to speak casually to several people there at the chapel, just mingling and getting to know others. Some people asked him how he knew Janet, and they were surprised to hear that he was the officer assigned her file and that he never met her before. Even the bank manager from the Canadian Imperial Bank of Commerce was there and she was impressed that Steven had come to the service. After about thirty minutes of socializing, Steven said goodbye to Marylin and thanked her for inviting him before he excused himself. Once again, she thanked him for taking the time on his day off to come there for her sister. Clearly, Marylin was appreciated for taking care of this service for Janet. From what Steven heard, Janet was very well-respected by all those in attendance and by all who knew her too.

With the memorial service now over, Steven left in his pickup truck to go and grab some dinner with a group of guys he hung out with outside of his work. The group tended to meet nearly every Friday evening at a local family-owned Italian restaurant, but as Steven worked a strange pattern of two days followed by two nights, then four days off, he could not always join them at this festive gathering of men. He only met them for the first time after he moved to Prince George just a short time before, but they welcomed him with open arms and made him feel like a brother of theirs right from the very start. This Friday evening it would work out for him to get together with this group of friends that affectionately called themselves a 'motley crew of reprobates.'

This group always commented that they were meeting together to make good men even better. But considering the teasing they did with each other; the casual observer might not believe it at first. But they were all brothers at heart. Some of these men were the same men that Steven had asked to come with him the next day to assist with helping Ed. When Steven asked for some of them to come for part of the day to Summit Lake, there were some who could not come due to prior commitments, but others who said yes right away. But tonight, there were far more men at this dinner than would be joining him the next morning. He didn't need more than about four more people to join him the following morning.

This family restaurant served them pizza's and other Italian foods. They always welcomed this group despite the fact that they could be a little noisy. The staff knew that they were all good people and that noise wasn't a reflection on their character. The owners knew that on Friday night, they should push together some tables at the back of the restaurant and that there would frequently be between fifteen and twenty of them showing up just for this group alone. Sometimes there were even more attending, but rarely less unless the weather was really bad that day, or it was a holiday. At least once or twice a year the group would advise the restaurant staff that the following week, many of them would be bringing their wives and girlfriends too. It could get very busy for the staff, but they always appreciated the business despite the elevated sound level in the restaurant. Likewise, if the service was a little slower on these exceptionally busy days, these guys would never complain, and they were always nice to the servers and staff. They ensured that every time they came, the servers would get a decent tip to reflect how they enjoyed the staff and food there.

The conversation was always pleasant, and as Steven was still very new in this group, he found himself to be the focus of everyone there wanting to get to know him better. They took great interest in where he was raised, and how his new career is going. He wanted to get to know them better too, but as he was the new one, and there were so many of them, it would take some time. But at least he could see some of them the following day when they go to Summit Lake.

After another nice meal and good conversation with his friends at the restaurant, they all started to slowly depart for their respective homes, spouses and girlfriends. Those joining Steven the following day discussed the idea of taking two vehicles to the older man's cabin the next morning. Also discussed by them was what tools and items they would need to be brought along with them. Steven suggested that in addition to the door jam and lock needing to be fixed, there were likely other routine repairs to be done around this cabin.

The next morning, they all planned to meet at a convenient location next to a building with a big parking lot so that they could carpool using just the two vehicles. Steven had in the bed of his pick-up truck all the items that he and others thought they might need to do these repairs. So, he could only have one passenger upfront in his cab. There was also a little bit of lumber and paint to assist in repairing the door jam. The remaining people were in the other vehicle. Some others brought the usual hammer and other handy tools to do whatever work they could with what they brought. Before leaving from home, he warmed up some Costco penne alfredo with chicken that he previously purchased for this day's work. He guessed that three of the meals should do. He placed them into a cooler to keep it warm for lunch, along with paper plates and plastic cutlery. The cooler was also rated for keeping things warm, so he was certain it would still be hot enough to enjoy at lunch time. He placed the cooler in the front of his truck so it would be warmer than in the bed. There were also cans of beverages, but those he left in the bed of his truck to keep cool.

    Before they met at the parking lot, Steven had picked up coffees for everyone at the local Tim Hortons. He knew that they would all appreciate it as much as he did. One was a tea drinker, so it was a good thing Steven asked them all what they wanted before he got to the coffee shop.

    Shortly after the group met up at the parking lot, everyone got into the two vehicles and they left and proceeded north on the highway towards Summit Lake. The roads were a little better on this day compared to when Steven got the call while at work a few days before. Possibly this was due to the fact that the sun was up at this time today, and on Steven's previous trip, being much earlier, it was still dark when he started out and when the sun did come up, it was an overcast day. Still driving safely, due to the winter road conditions, the drive took them about forty-five minutes when both vehicles arrived at Ed's cabin. From the cabin, Ed had heard the vehicles pull up and opened the front door to greet them.

When the others exited the first vehicle, Steven was surprised to hear them all talk to Ed like they knew him for years. He was certain that he never even told any of them his name, yet clearly, they all seemed to know Ed even though he lived in Surrey down near Vancouver. One even joked to Ed that had he known it was him he was coming to help; he would have slept in that day instead. It was obvious to Steven that all his friends not only knew Ed but also liked and deeply respected him too.

After a couple of minutes exchanging comments about how Ed has been doing, the group didn't take long to get right to the work on the various repairs and cabin upkeep. Steven and one other person were working on repairing the door frame and the door, while some of the others were doing various minor repairs inside and one of them was even reattaching the gutter that was coming off the eves of the cabin. The door frame was replaced with new boards including very long screws that anchored the frame securely to the outside walls of the cabin. Now Steven felt this cabin was much more secure. Steven wondered if he should have brought a few more boards with him, but they ended up not needing any more materials. He had just enough lumber for the door and the door jam, along with a new replacement board behind the front gutter, plus a couple of other repairs inside the cabin. The paint that one of them brought didn't quite match the original grey shade, but it was doubtful that Ed would even care about that. After all, this was just a cabin that he occasionally visited, and it was a little weathered, to begin with. Fortunately, the group would leave it in much better repair now that there were a couple of minor fixes completed.

Only about one hour after the group started and all the work was done at the cabin. Of course, the group stayed a short while longer to enjoy a fresh pot of hot coffee that Ed had put on for them along with the still hot lunch that Steven had brought. One of them even commented to Ed that the coffee was so good it was worth the drive and the work they did just for a cup of it. Ed joked that it must be the fact that he spiked the pot. The conversation was upbeat with the usual friendly verbal jabs at one another. These were the type of verbal assaults that only proved how much they appreciated one another. After the clean up, Steven advised Ed that he likely had two more meals worth of the chicken penne alfredo pasta that he would leave for him to enjoy.

Some more time had passed after the final cleanup and last cups of coffee were consumed. The group of guys were preparing to leave when Ed asked Steven if he had any information on why that lady had killed herself. The others not knowing anything about this, asked about what had happened.

All Steven could really say was that all his inquiries led him to believe that being a widow, she had fallen on hard times financially due to a romance scam, and she must have felt a combination of extreme destitution and shame for believing in the scammer who took from her all the money he could. He did tell Ed and the group that the victim was taken for all the assets she had and was therefore completely destitute and even soon to lose her home. He even went on to suggest that the sister of the victim is going to be struggling just to pay for the funeral as there is nothing left in the estate that Janet left behind.

The other men there, hearing this for the first time, felt sad for her situation despite not knowing anything about her. One of them had even commented that he could see why someone would feel shame, but that she really shouldn't as the scam was probably pulled off by a very clever con artist. He went on to talk about how when frogs are sitting in water that is slowly being brought to a boil, they do not realize that the water is too hot, and they never jump out to save themselves. Steven thought that was a good analogy as to how Janet likely got swindled out of all her money, but he dared not ask this guy how he knew this. Perhaps he was once a victim too? Steven didn't want to dig up anything that someone had worked hard to bury. If indeed this is what happened. But he would wonder about this.

With all the chores and repairs now done both inside and outside of the cabin and the coffee and lunch now finished, they were getting ready to leave when one said to Ed, "happy to meet and sorry to part," As he gave him a friendly bear hug. With that said, they all prepared to leave.

As Steven was about to get into his pick-up truck, Ed came up to him and pulled him aside for a moment. He handed Steven an envelope he said contained a cheque and asked him quietly; "please give this to her sister to assist in paying for the funeral expenses."

Steven was taken back; he could take the cheque and give it to Marylin as he was not in receipt of anything against RCMP policy. So, he thanked Ed for the thoughtful donation and took the envelope and left. Steven felt at a loss for words over the generosity he saw in Ed. He had no idea how much was in the envelope, but he figured no matter what the amount, that this was a display of true generosity and selflessness and Steven felt almost like the gift was indirectly for him too. Right after that he and Jorge got into Stevens pickup truck, and the remainder got into the car, and the two vehicles headed south to make their way back south to Prince George.

Jorge was a new friend of Steven that he met shortly after he was posted to Prince George right out of RCMP Depot training. They had really only known each other for about two or three weeks. But it was obvious that they would be long-time friends. He was the person that Steven had contacted at the electronics shop for help with Janet's computer. So, he thought it would be a good opportunity to talk to him about how he has Janet's computer back at his home now, and just what he should do with it and how he should search things.

Jorge was a relatively recent immigrant from Mexico where he was previously a practicing criminal lawyer. But now having great technical skills, he works at a computer shop. But Jorge's real goal is to open his own drywalling business. Computers were just a hobby, but he had the drywalling skills for a long time. He was very helpful in rebuilding Ed's door frame and specifically in rehanging the front door of the cabin.

It was during the drive back to Prince George that Jorge suggested to Steven that he trace all the IP addresses of each email coming from someone who is suspected by Steven of participating in this scam. Of course, this could take several weeks or even months to do, but there may be a pattern of where the emails are originating from. This pattern may end up possibly revealing something, or maybe not. But it would be prudent to do this despite how time-consuming it is. Steven would need to create a running log of all his findings from the search.

Jorge also suggested that Steven should read all the email messages that Janet received. He should be viewing each one carefully to look specifically at the language and in particular how things are being said in these messages. Steven would need to pay attention to certain spelling mistakes or speech styles. If they suddenly change, it is likely to indicate that there is a different person writing the emails as if they are Benjamin. This may also be verified by the IP addresses of the emails received by her. With these two pieces of key information, it may be possible for Steven to ascertain the precise number of people who are impersonating this soldier and who swindled Janet out of her money. There would likely be others involved behind the scenes, but from this information, all that could be determined in the numbers was just how many had personally conversed with Janet. Of course, Steven wanted to learn all this and much more, but this was a great starting point despite the huge amount of work it would create for him.

The other suggestion that was made by Jorge was to look at where Janet was asked to send the money transfers to Benjamin. If it was all at the same location, that would tell him that there is an accomplice likely in that city he was told of. If it was different locations, this would be important information too. This, of course, would add more than one person into the entire scam. Although even at this point, it was probably that there are many more people behind the scenes that Steven would ever know about. This was also eluded to by Robert with RCMP Criminal Intelligence Program.

It was during this drive back to Prince George that Steven finally realized to what extent the investigation would entail and just how much work was involved in this. He knew that once he started this work, he would not be finished for a considerable amount of time, likely even months before completion. But even with the knowledge of how much work it would entail, Steven still wanted to learn what he could and to work as hard as he could to be a voice for Janet. Even though Steven knew it would never result in a conviction for anyone, he still wanted to see if he could prevent someone else from this horrible situation that Janet was put through. But maybe with a little luck, he could help shut down some scammers and keep someone else from being swindled out of their life savings.

Chapter Four

Once the two of them returned from Summit Lake back to the parking lot in Prince George, Steven dropped Jorge off at his vehicle and he proceeded to drive over to Marylin's home to present her with the envelope that Ed had asked him to pass on to her. He knocked on her door and she came and answered it looking a little puzzled by his appearance knowing he was on his days off.

Steven explained to her that he and some new friends of his went to see the gentleman who discovered the break-in to assist in some minor repairs on his cabin. Marylin knew from Steven that Janet was the cause of some of the damage, but that the cabin owner felt a real sadness for her and was not upset at Janet for the small amount of damage done.

Marylin was stunned that an officer would go that far on his day off to assist someone he only met once. Steven knew this was unusual for a police officer to do, but he didn't do it based on his job as a RCMP officer, he did it based on the brotherhood of helping each other out and always striving to be a better person. It was a code he lived by, as did his friends who assisted him.

Steven explained to her that the older man heard from him about her unexpected costs for her sister's funeral service and that he wanted to help her out and so he gave Steven this envelope that he now presented to Marylin.

Steven had no idea what the amount of the cheque was, so he was eager to see her open the envelope to learn the amount. No matter what the amount, he thought that was very generous of Ed. He didn't need to do that, but this was a true reflection of just what kind of a man he really is.

Naturally Marylin was very surprised at learning how someone she had never met, could be so thoughtful to both her and her deceased sister. With the envelope handed to her, she opened it up and removed the cheque. Almost immediately she had tears forming in her eyes from the generosity of a man she had never even met, nor even heard of before a few days ago. It was only today that she even learned his name was Edward, which she saw on the cheque. Once the envelope was opened, Steven learned that Ed had given her five thousand dollars. Marylin commented that it was almost the exact amount that she had to pay for the funeral service and cremation. Steven felt so glad that he had taken this day to assist Ed. It turned out to help so many more than just one man. Steven could see firsthand how the generosity of Ed made such a big difference on others and this included himself too, because he got the honor or seeing this firsthand and his work at the cabin was now more of a privilege he got to do than it ever was a chore. Steven also had to fight the tears from forming in his eyes when he thought of what a nice and kind thing Ed did for her, and how he was so fortunate to be a part of it. Deep down Steven laughed at himself for this being the first time he fought back tears since he was a little boy, but when it was for a good reason like this, it sure wasn't a sign of weakness, but true happiness at seeing the good in others.

Steven learned through his training that it was common for police officers to lose faith in humanity from all the negative things they see. He also knew that when this starts to happen to him, he can draw on this to always keep him squared away.

Steven left Marylin's home shortly after that, and he returned to his truck to head back to his home, but before he put his vehicle in gear, he sat there a moment thinking about what had just happened. He laughed to himself at the thought of how the tears forming in his eyes, under these circumstances, could never been a shot at his own toughness. He was a compassionate man and he hoped he always will be. After a couple more minutes, he put his truck in drive and headed home.

Later that evening, long after he returned home from Marylin's, Steven was worried that Ed gave her that much money out of a sense of guilt because it was his shotgun that was used by Janet to kill herself, but a call to one of the others in the group confirmed this was just the type of man Ed was. He cared deeply for others, yet smart enough and discerning enough not to let himself get swindled. So, with this relief in Steven's mind, he set up Marylin's computer using his own monitor, keyboard, and mouse. He turned it on and connected it to the internet so that when he looked at Janet's emails, he could run the IP trace on each one of them individually.

One by one Steven brought up her emails and read them each carefully. He created detailed notes on each one about its contents, speech style, noted spelling mistakes etc. Then he ran an IP trace on the emails individually, starting with the oldest one first and working slowly towards the most current one. It didn't take long to learn which emails he could ignore in her inbox. He had no interest in reading anything not pertaining to this case. He Immediately saw that he could pass on ones from the bank or businesses. There were also some from friends that he learned had nothing to do with his search, so he ignored those ones too and concentrated primarily with the ones from the man or men he suspected in the romance scam.

With each email from him, Steven would copy the routing information and paste it into a search engine specifically for tracing IP addresses. Then he would take the results and copy them into a word document that would eventually list all the emails in chronological order, along with all the details already mentioned, along with the date and time it was sent. Steven worked for nearly two hours but realized that he had hardly made a dent in the vast number of emails in total.

He continued working for a good three hours logging all the particulars of the emails before his eyes started to bother him and he thought about stopping for the night. But just before logging off the computer for the night, he started noting if he thought there was a change in who was writing these emails to Janet, just like Jorge suggested he should do. But Steven was so enthralled in his work that he never noticed how much time was passing by. He pressed on and found so much more. Finally, he managed to step away from the computer and head off to bed. His eyes were sore, and he was tired.

One of the key pieces of information contained in the earlier emails that he did notice and that he thought was interesting is that all of those emails showed an IP address that appeared to come from London England. As he read through them, Steven thought to himself that 'this person was a really smooth talker. He clearly had the gift of a silver tongue who undoubtedly said to her all the right things to get Janet to fall in love with the fictitious person that he wanted to portray to her'.

The story that this scammer was feeding Janet was that he was a Major in the United States Army and he used the name 'Benjamin Yardley'. He was currently on deployment in Afghanistan where he had been for three months into his ten-month long deployment. He told her that he was at a 'forward operating base' (FOB) in the Korengal Valley which is known for being one of the most dangerous areas during the campaign against the Taliban. Steven had to wonder if the scammers knew where the real soldier had died because this was the same area. He believed this information was told to Janet to keep her a little worried all the time and of course to eagerly anticipate every email that would arrive from 'Benjamin' anytime he was able to get to a computer with an internet connection.

The person posing as Benjamin talked about the loneliness of the battlefield, and the extreme responsibility he has to his subordinate men. The long hours of boredom followed by short times of intense terror, all this information was meant to help focus Janet's mind on being fearful for him as well as develop a sense of loyalty and pride in him at the same time.

He went on to tell her about how scared he was now that he was sometimes being shot at. And of course, there was the constant fear of improvised explosive devises (IED's) being detonated near him, or worse of all; capture and being tortured to death by the Taliban while being video recorded to be broadcast on the internet for family and friends of the victim to see.

Of course, the very real fear of capture was likely the biggest fear of the real soldiers in these parts. It was a near-certain horrible death sentence. If you were not beaten and tortured to death, which was a horrible way for anyone to die, the Taliban sometimes videoed the beheading of soldiers to show on the internet as a warning to others. Often times, the Taliban would then parade the deceased soldier through the towns and villages while further degrading the corpse. The level of cruelty of the Taliban members was beyond what others could comprehend. All this in the name of a religion that they claim is peaceful and just. Maybe true Islam is, but these people sure were not practicing what they preached. It was clear that this person or people who was posing as 'Benjamin' knew exactly what to say to Janet in order to keep her worrying so much about him and his safety. But it all started out much more civilized and peaceful. It reminded Steven of his friend's comment of the frog in water slowly brought to a boil. Once again, he thought, 'what a great analogy that was'.

This person, or more accurately these people also repeatedly told Janet that it was her emails and her caring messages that kept him going through all this danger and horror. It was the love that they shared for each other that gave him reasons to be more careful when dealing with the enemy. The author of this email even stated how happy he was to have finally met his soul mate. These were well-chosen words to make her feel loved by Benjamin, as well as to want to help him in any way she could. After all, she believed that it was her encouraging words that assisted in him maintaining a safer attitude in his work. Building on these emotions that they implanted in Janet would be useful to them later on in the next phase of their scam.

Steven couldn't help but feel that these emails were so slick in getting her prepared to feel guilty if she didn't send him money when that request finally came in. 'Benjamin' was really setting her up for this scam. Steven could clearly see why Marylin said that Janet had a whole new outlook a few months back. This scammer was clearly winning her heart over. Clearly, she was falling in love with who she thought Benjamin was, and Steven could easily see why. The silver tongue worked well on her as it would on most people.

As he was spending a considerable amount of time reading these emails from Benjamin to Janet, Steven could really understand how she got pulled into this scam. He thought to himself that many people could fall for this, male or female, gay or straight. Combined with the fact that she is lonely as a relatively recent widow, wanting to find her ideal man, and then believing she had done so and the hook was now set for them to start asking for money from her. But it wouldn't happen just yet. Still, Steven could read from the email's just how loving and caring Janet really is. He thought to himself that people must be complete monsters to prey on the kindness of good people like Janet. He truly felt a sadness for her. But this sadness only reinforced the very reasons Steven undertook to learn everything he could about them and in particular, this very scam.

Before the people posing as Benjamin started asking her for money, they needed to build up the story even more. Steven read on and found that Benjamin had now slightly changed the story. His new claim was that he was with the 'Army National Guard' not the US Army that he had at first said and he got called up to go to Afghanistan. When the two first started communicating, Benjamin said he was with the 'Army', but most people wouldn't consider this change of fact misleading, it would be viewed merely as semantics that didn't amount to much. But in fact, they were critical in the story that was being laid out for Janet. He claimed that he was from Phoenix Arizona and that he had a really nice house in a good area there, complete with a swimming pool in the back yard and a large saguaro cactus out in the front of his adobe home on the north west corner of the city. Benjamin was required to leave his higher paying job to serve his country. Outside of the military, he claimed to be working as a logistics manager with a large national industrial machine shipping company. Now working just for the National Guard, he could barely make his mortgage payments. But once he gets sent back home, he can return to his former job and resume being financially well off and self-sufficient all over again. This story not only showed him as a patriot willing to give up so much for his country, but it also set the stage for his need for money too.

Steven thought to himself that if he didn't know any better, this would be a story that almost everyone would find very believable. Most people care about others, especially the soldiers who they view as doing a dangerous job for the benefit of their country and for their fellow citizens. Clearly, if this fabricated story was, in fact, true, Benjamin would be deserving of the assistance from the very people he is fighting for. But Steven had the benefit of knowing this was all a ruse to separate Janet from her money. This further angered Steven as he was also very pro-military and saw it as an attack on the legitimate soldiers who were on deployment too. After all, they deserve the respect of the citizens of the country they represent along with their allied partners. This type of scam just helps build distrust for the military members who did nothing wrong at all. Steven always liked the idea of the military, and his back up plan if he did not get into the RCMP was to hopefully join the air force.

Coincidently an email had now come in that was asking for a $5000 loan from Janet. This was also when the IP address had changed from London England, to an IP address now showing in Toronto Canada. That was something that Steven made a note of right on the word document log sheet he was creating. This indicated that the group was using one email address per pseudonym even though it was likely many people impersonating the same man. Obviously, he discovered a key piece of a very huge puzzle. First the London connection, and now Toronto one; he wondered what would he find next?

With more research conducted, Steven noticed that the money was to be sent to a Western Union located in Las Vegas Nevada. It was a very good back story that was used by them to get Janet to send them money. The Western Union locations in Las Vegas were likely some of the busier ones for getting money sent too due to people loosing more then they planned when gambling. The story these people used was that 'Benjamin' had left a high paying job because he was called up to work for the Army National Guard for nearly one year. During that time, he struggled to make his mortgage payments from what little the National Guard paid him while he was on deployment.

With the military now being in arrears with Benjamin's regular pay, he is now left in a debt situation with the mortgage holder for his home in Phoenix Arizona. Steven thought this was a very believable story, especially after a long time conversing where trust is built up over an extended period of time building that trust. The other thing that caught Steven's attention was that he asked Janet to use a password for the money to be picked up as his sister had lost her identification recently.

A quick internet look into this idea confirmed that with a verbal password used, it is easy to do money transfers to any location of the Western Union without the need to be showing any identification at all. Steven was surprised to learn this, but it made sense to him because if someone was traveling and got robbed of all their money, credit cards and identification, they could still obtain money from family or friends far away by using a password or phrase to have the cash released to them.

It was not long after that that the money transfer had taken place. It was the next day that Steven saw that Janet had received the anticipated gratitude email that anyone giving the loan would expect to receive. It talked about how grateful he was for her to save his home and how this clearly showed him how much she loved him. There were also the comments about how lucky he was to have found such a wonderful and beautiful lady as Janet. The email went on to tell her how he thinks about her constantly when he is in battle zones. The comment that really struck Steven was when he said that she is the reason he is careful in battle. There was even that promise that when his time in Afghanistan is over, they will always be together.

Steven thought to himself about how these people operate. These guys are very good at saying what their victims clearly desire to hear. They are smooth talkers and they are a well-rehearsed and organized group. They know how to win the girl over and how to gain her trust and show appreciation even though it is all a big con job. They could teach phycologists a thing or too about how relationships could work. But Steven couldn't help but feel a melancholy once again for poor Janet. It was obvious from these emails that she sent to him, that she really loved and cared for who she thought Major Benjamin Yardley really was.

But now while reading all of these emails she received, Steven was getting even more mad at them for what they have done to Janet. Despite not knowing her, or even having even meet her, he was starting to know what her personality was like and he liked who she was. Now he felt an intense anger for these people who harmed her so badly. In his mind, morally this was clearly a case of murder, even though legally it would not meet the test. He always hated it when injustices are done to anyone, which is one of the reasons he wanted to become a police officer. And he was also very upset at these people for causing this harm to Janet and others like her. But now after spending so much time reading these emails and learning about how caring and nice Janet was and how evil these men really are, he wanted to see them caught and held accountable. He also knew that this was very unlikely to happen. But what surprised Steven the most is that he was even learning some things about himself by doing this investigation.

He learned that he was far more compassionate and caring than he realized. He always knew he was, but this reinforced it. Also, after Ed gave a cheque to Marylin, he felt that it was indirectly a gift to him too, because he learned how caring he really was and saw how a small act of service helping out a newly met friend could assist in such a large way that he could never anticipate.

Another thing that made Steven mad was that some people may put part of the blame on Janet for allowing herself to be deceived. Perhaps this could be blamed on her by simply being naïve? Maybe. But Steven thought they were so smooth that many people, both male, and female could easily be caught up in this type of scam, even people who were not so naïve could be loured into trusting this well practised group. He was not accusing her of being naïve, but at first, he did feel that way. Now as he was reading the emails, he could clearly see how easy it was for people to become their victims. This was obviously a well practiced routine done by skilled conmen who slowly lured Janet into a feeling of being in love as well as a developed trust for who she though this person really was. The more he learned about how this scam went down, the more Steven thought he should acquire further information about romance scams in general.

Steven needed to take a break from all the reading and logging of vast number of these emails. He had been working diligently for so many hours yet had hardly even put a dent in the number left to investigate. So, he put aside this task for a while and deciding that he wanted to learn more about these online scams, the first thing he did was an internet search using the phrase 'romance scams.' It was there that he found several good articles on this topic and even some tragic stories that were posted online. He was reading many of them trying to learn more than what he already had learned from Robert with the RCMP Criminal Intelligence Program, but it did not really increase his knowledge too much. Suddenly amongst all the online articles he saw something that really caught his attention, there amongst the different articles was something Steven didn't expect to see at all in his research. In fact, he looked at it for a long time for him to be certain of what he saw.

There was an arrest of a Nigerian man in Toronto. He was charged with being part of a romance scam organization whereby he took advantage of a lady in a rural town in Ontario and convinced her to send him $20,000. Steven read the article and was disgusted with how this man also took advantage of another caring lady. But the part that really caught his attention and almost took the wind out of him was when Steven scrolled down the page. It was there that he came across the photo of the accused man. Steven knew instantly that it was the same black man he had seen at the funeral just the day before. His name showed up on the web page as Inegdebion Tinubu, which he learned is a Nigerian term meaning 'family supports me'. When Steven learned his name and the meaning, his immediate thought was 'nice family'. He is a Nigerian citizen here as an immigrant with a Canada Permanent Resident card. Likely he has been in Canada under five years, but that could not be determined, nor did it really matter except that he was not a Canadian citizen according to the article.

Steven knew that once he returns to work following his days off, he would need to call Robert at RCMP Criminal Intelligence Program in the Vancouver area office for a second time. This was potentially a pretty big discovery for him. Actually, Steven decided right then that this information was far too important to wait for his scheduled return to work. Sure, it might not have made a big difference, but Steven wouldn't know that for sure until he had a chance to talk to Robert. This had the Potential for being huge information, so he needed to pass it on sooner rather than later. He would let the investigators determine if it was critical or not, but in case it was, it would be best to pass it on as soon as possible. So, based on the implications of this new discovery, he would go in a few days before the start of his four-day rotation and call Robert first thing tomorrow morning. He thought that this might not be a good thing to put off until his normal return to work, even if for just two more days. As today was Sunday, he knew that Robert would not likely be at work now, so it would have to wait until the following day regardless. But he would ensure that he passed on this new information at the earliest opportunity.

Even though Steven had no idea how useful this information would be to Robert and the RCMP Criminal Intelligence Program, he still felt like this was a huge accomplishment making this kind of discovery. But until he could get to the office the next morning, he would continue his reading on romance scams and the Black Axe group that caused so much pain and sadness to so many victims, directly or indirectly.

Chapter Five

So, Steven came into the Police Station on Monday morning just as he had previously planned to do. It seemed that not one of the other constables and office staff from the other shifts even noticed that he was there on a day off, it was either that or they never really cared as they probably assumed that he was there to work on some files he wanted to close before his supervisor came down on him, which might actually be a good idea. It was as if this was perfectly normal for police to want to be there on their off days. As he was a bit early, he went to review the crime stats over the past few days and was shocked to see that there was a break and enter at Janet's home that was reported this past Saturday. Steven went to a computer to review the file to see what he could learn. It seems it had occurred between five in the afternoon on Friday and eight in the morning on Saturday two days prior. The constables who attended her home had noted in their report that the only thing that seemed missing was the computer from her desk. There was nothing else that appeared to be taken or even seemed out of place to the attending constable. Of course, Steven had the computer at his home, so he brought up the digital file and saw that it did link to his file. He noted this piece of information on both files so that the missing computer's location is known and that it will no longer be listed as possibly stolen. He worried that he could be in trouble for having the computer but figured that the ends justified the means and he would worry about that at a later time. Of course, being a probationary constable, this did worry him too.

By about 9:00 that morning he decided it was time to give Robert a phone call down at the RCMP Criminal Intelligence Program office. Many officers were now out on the road at this time, so it was easy for him to find an available desk that offered a small amount of privacy. He looked up the number he had phoned just the other day, and it was picked up on the second ring. He asked to speak to Robert and a moment later, the two were on the phone line together.

"Robert, this is Steven Browne here from the Prince George Detachment. We spoke last week."

"Steven, yes I recall talking to you the other day. How are things in the Great White North doing? You know I started my RCMP carrier in Prince George too."

"Was it as cold then as it is now?"

"Colder; how have you been doing?"

I am doing pretty good. But there was a strange turn to this situation. I thought I would run it by you."

"Okay, talk to me, I am all ears. Then I will tell you about my experience in Prince George."

"So, on Friday evening I attended the funeral of the victim who committed suicide. While there I saw what I would have to describe as a Nigerian looking man in attendance. He walked into the funeral chapel during the last few minutes of the service, look around at every person there and then he leaves in a hurry the moment the service ended. What caught my attention is that he really seemed out of place, so I watched him intently. "

"Your Spidey senses were tingling huh?"

"Very much so. There was something so out-of-place about him. So, lets fast forward to Saturday night. I was looking online about romance scams and low and behold I see an online news article about a man charged with this type of crime in Toronto. Guess what? I believe it was the same guy who showed up in Prince George for the funeral service."

"Let me guess; he came into the service and had a good look around. He then picked up a leaflet from the service for this lady and then he quickly left as soon as the memorial service was over?"

"That is exactly what he did. I went a minute later out the main door to see where he was going, but I never did spot him again. There were vehicles on the road and a bus leaving the area, so there was no way for me to know where he went."

"Send me the guys name and I will look into it more. I may need to contact the officer who has conduct of this file in Toronto and likely the Crown Counsel lawyer dealing with it there too."

"His name is Inegbedion", stated Steven

"Oh yes, I think I know that name. If it is who I think he is, he is a very nasty piece of work."

"There was one other thing to tell you. On Friday, the deceased victim's home was broken into, the time frame of the break-in was from about an hour before to about two hours after the victim's funeral. The police report says that it appeared that nothing but the victim's computer was taken, and nothing else seemed out of place to the officer who took the call. Of course, I have that computer at my home. I hope I do not get into trouble for that."

"Why do you have the computer? And, why is it at your home?"

"I thought it would be interesting to search through every email in there from this possible Black Axe group. I am tracing the IP addresses of each email individually to see where they originated from, and after talking to you, I was interested to see how they sweet talk her into handing over all of her money."

"I am glad I interested you enough to do your own research. I am betting that whoever did that break in was specifically looking for that computer, and likely nothing else. You need to look at the contents of that computer very carefully. I would bet there is something incriminating located on it. As for you getting into trouble having that computer in your home, if you are called in to a supervisor's office about it, you tell them that I suggested you do this as a favor for me, but that you should do this on your own time. I am not worried about them raising this issue with me," replied Robert.

"Thank you so much, Robert. I owe you one."

"Not at all, with the information you just gave me, I think we can safely say we are even. But now I want to tell you about my carrier. I was a civilian employee of the RCMP, having just finished my education as radio technician. I was building custom made radio bugging devices for the RCMP Criminal Intelligence Program when my peers here I thought I should apply as a regular member. So, I did and in no time, I was sent to Regina. I had to do my mandatory year on uniform work, so I was sent to Prince George as my first posting too."

"I bet Prince George has changed quite a bit since you were here."

"No doubt. Back then when we pulled people over for speeding, they still used the old paper drivers' licenses. It was a long time ago, and I am nearing the end of my long career. Back then you would unfold the drivers license and often the person would fold a twenty-dollar bill inside it. It was a non-verbal way of attempting to bribe the officer into not writing the ticket. I recall this one time getting the paper and opening up the license and discovering the money. I asked the driver if it was his and he said no. So, I crumpled it up and threw it on the ground. After I wrote him the ticket, I saw him get out of the car and pick up the twenty. I never laughed so hard in my life."

Steven had to laugh too as he could clearly see in his minds eye the story unfolding. Shortly after this they disconnected the call.

With that phone call now done, Steven decided to head back home and enjoy the remainder of his day off. Of course, he couldn't resist going back on to Janet's computer for some more email investigation. His interest in what he might find was only growing stronger with each and every new discovery.

On Wednesday morning Steven arrived at work at the start of his four days on - four days off rotation. He got there early to give him time to put on his uniform as well as check his email. Then after the usual morning briefing, he spent a short time doing his routine pre-trip inspection on the police car that he would be using that day.

After updating some notations in the files on Janet, he left the office and started a patrol in his routine area. He decided at about 8:00 that morning to set up by a school to catch people driving too fast in a school zone. Of course, nearly every community everywhere had the same problem of speeders near children, and it will never go away no matter how many tickets he could write. He waited at an intersection and it didn't take him long to pull over the first offender. He probably wrote about five tickets and was ready to set up again for the sixth one, but shortly after completing the last ticket, he got a call from his dispatcher to RTO which meant for him to return to the office. He was about twenty minutes away from the station. Once he arrived, he was asked to phone a detective with the Toronto Police Service. This only came as a mild surprise to Steven based on the sighting that he had of their suspect a just a few days before.

Once again, he sat down at an available desk and made the phone call. When it was picked up, he asked to speak to Detective Adrian Holland and shortly after he was put through to his desk.

"Detective Adrian Holland here," replied the man who picked up the phone.

"Hello, this is constable Steven Browne from Prince George in British Columbia here. I had a message to give you a call."

"Yes, your associate Robert with the RCMP Criminal Intelligence Program called me a while ago and told me that you may have seen a suspect from Ontario who is facing charges for an internet fraud case I am working on. I would like to send you some pictures to look at and if you can tell me it was the same person. I have already emailed you them, if you could please have a look."

With that email waiting for him, Steven advised him that he is now logging onto the computer and it will only take a moment or two. "Yes, I see I have an email from you. I am just opening the email now."

"Great. Please look at those pictures, are they the man you saw?"

"I am quite certain that he is the same individual I saw at the funeral on Friday. So, he is the guy that is charged with the romance fraud?"

"Yes, not only that, after I spoke to Robert, I called a couple of different airlines and confirmed he flew to Prince George for that one night." This probably won't tie him in with the death you are dealing with, but I would bet my paycheque that these cases are very much connected. Listen, I am going to forward this information on to the Crown Counsel office here in Toronto, they now have conduct of this file. I am thinking that he will probably contact you soon with their own set of questions."

"Thank you for letting me know. If there is anything more I can do from here, don't hesitate to ask."

"Excellent. If I need you, I will call, and vise versa."

With that information passed on, Steven then hung up the phone and left to go back on the road for the remainder of his shift. When he got back to his car there was a call pending on his mobile computer for a shoplifting offense at a local sporting goods store. He decided to take that call before the dispatcher assigned it to him anyway, so off he went.

The remainder of the shift could best be described as routine. There were the usual calls, traffic stops, and of course, the never-ending report writing.

That evening after Steven got off work, he went home and made dinner for himself while booting up Janet's computer. He knew this would likely be his home routine for some time as he needed to read and trace every single email he could find on Janet's computer from these scammers, and there were so many of these emails too, he had hardly managed to check a small percentage of them, yet he has been working diligently at this for a few days now.

It wasn't until two more days had passed that Steven was about to start the last two shifts prior to his four days off, these were the overnight shifts and made Steven tired for about a good day into his days off. He showed up to work with plenty of time to change into his uniform and read any alerts that may be posted for officers to peruse. There were just normal alerts for the constables to look for. Pay attention to these two guys who are theft from auto suspects, or that guy who likes to tag everything he can with a can of spray paint. Some of these graffiti artists have real talent, yet most do not. But in any case, doing this without the permission of the property owner is a crime even if they do think they are a greater artist than Pablo Picasso. Steven laughed silently to himself when he thought about this one place that he heard about that was targeted by a talented graffiti artist. After he was caught sometime later, and identified as the suspect, the business owner refused to press charges as his business improved with the new mural that magically appeared on the side of his store. Of course, this was the exception, not the rule.

Before leaving the station and heading out on the road to begin his patrols, Steven logged into the desktop computer and he was only a little surprised to see an email waiting for him from the crown counsel office in Toronto. In the email, Steven was asked to call Paul Barker at his office at his earliest convenience. But Steven figured it was too late in the evening in Toronto. But why not call and see if he was still in his office as he may like to work late. This lawyer may be the type of person who works very long hours. Many crown lawyers do, but some prefer to start very early too.

Steven was not surprised when there was no answer to the call. He thought about leaving a voice mail but decided that he would return to the office around five in the morning and call shortly after that as this crown lawyer will likely be in the office then.

After the usual start of shift routine, Steven left the RCMP parking lot and thought about going to see Marylin to give her an update. Then thinking through it, he decided not too. There really was not much that he could tell her yet. Certainly, he could not tell her of the information about his recent discovery. So, he would wait until he had more to tell her; or things that specifically linked to her sister.

Steven decided it would be a good idea to park his police his car at Janet's home and go knock on some neighbors' doors to ask if anyone saw anything to do with the recent break-in on the past Friday. One of the neighbours did tell him of seeing a guy who looked out of place in their neighbourhood during that Friday evening a few nights before. Steven asked the lady what seemed out of place about him and he could tell immediately that this lady seemed uncomfortable voicing her reasons why. With a little prompting, Steven was able to learn that she was reluctant to say that the man she saw was black. She was concerned that telling him this fact could be viewed as racist. But Steven, supressing a little laughter, assured her that an identifying feature like his color is not a racist comment at all, yet he did appreciate the lady's reluctance. It showed her character and morals to him. But it was also true that describing a person by their race was no more racist than describing someone who has a scar or a tattoo. These were just identifying features.

Steven did learn from this witness that she thought the man was about thirty years old at the most, and 'very dark-skinned even for a black man', as she stated to him. And the thing that stood out the most to Steven was that her description of this man is that he looked African from what she understands them to look like, but not Jamaican. After noticing this man as being out of place in the neighbourhood, all she really saw from her vantage point was him walking away, so she never bothered to call the police because walking isn't a crime. She didn't even know that Janet's home was broken into until Steven showed up just a few minutes before. But she did hear through the neighbors that Janet was now deceased.

"I am curious, can you tell me what Janet was like?" Asked Steven

"She was such a nice lady. I often saw her out in the yard doing her gardening. She took real pride in having a nice garden with flowers and a manicured lawn. I talked to her a few times and it was obvious that she really cared about others too. I never knew her well before her husband died, but I always felt she had a deep sadness at her sudden loss. I always knew that she would do anything to find someone like him again. They must have had a very strong relationship. It was obvious to those who knew her that she was an exceptionally lonely lady after his unfortunate demise."

"She sounded like a very nice lady from everything I heard from people who knew her."

"She really was a lovely person. She had a true heart of gold. She was the type of person who would assist you in a heartbeat if you ever needed it. "

"Please tell me if you can, was she the type of person who could be taken advantage of easily?" Asked Steven.

"I hate to speak poorly of the dead, but I think she was a little naïve about how mean this world can really be. And maybe she cared, also, much about others as well. Sadly, not everyone deserved her benevolence. Therefore, she only saw the good in people. This was a nice quality about her, but if you ask me, a little foolish too."

"I am assuming based on what you have told me that yes, in fact you do think she can be taken advantage of. Would it have been easy for others to take advantage of her generosity?"

"Yes, I am afraid so. I hate to say it though."

With this information, Steven thanked her for her time talking to him and he returned to his car and back where he resumed his evening's patrols of the area assigned to him in this city.

So, Steven began by taking some calls that were pending from the dispatcher. The only calls that were waiting to be taken were the typical routine ones that regularly come in for a city like Prince George. He was relatively close to a call holding for some time. This was a vandalism call that was a low priority as whoever did it is long gone from the scene and there was never a suspect. So, he notified the dispatcher that he would take this call, and he was on his way to the location of the complaint.

He knew from the computer in the car that it was a vandalism call, but he did not know what type of vandalism. He attended the address expecting to find a keyed car or some other form of destruction. But it turned out that the property reference was complaining about 'another dumb-ass kid who tagged this fence'. This guy was hoping that an officer would have come by much sooner as he wanted to paint over the artwork prior to the sun going down. Now it was too late in the evening as the sun had disappeared hours ago. But Steven used his flashlight to look at the graffiti and suggested that he should not cover it up until he can get another officer to look at it and take a digital photograph for their records. The detachment had a constable whose secondary duties were to photograph and catalogue all the graffiti that he could that was done in and around the Prince George area. Each graffiti 'artist' had a unique style, and some had a unique signature too. Some of them really took pride in their work, so it was possible that this officer might be able to identify the 'artist' by his work and by his unique signature. The graffiti artists often had a signature that was a symbol or letters that created an alias name. But this officer would be able to identify the signature or work if he had it in his collection of photographs. Once positively identified there could be charges laid and possibly a civil action such as small claims court to paint over the work. But sometimes if there is a conviction, the judge could order the offender to pay restitution to those affected by his crime. Unfortunately, though this rarely happens because even in the unlikely event that the 'artist' could be identified, a conviction was a whole different matter.

The property owner liked the idea of catching the perpetrator but worried that leaving the graffiti up two more days may be harmful to the aesthetics of his home and neighborhood. The longer the graffiti remained on display, the more likely it would be for more graffiti to occur. After writing the report and making sure the officer who will come and photograph it for his files was copied on the police file, he continued his patrol of the neighbourhood. It wasn't long before other officers from his watch decided it was time to meet at a coffee shop for their first break of the shift.

The remainder of the shift was a typical routine night in Prince George. Steven was going from call to call until about midnight, then it started to slow down to where the officers might wish there was more to do. But this did give Steven time to finish off some outstanding reports before doing some more patrolling. He would park his car in a convenient location and begin typing out his various reports. Then at about five o'clock that morning, Steven decided it was time to head in and make that call to Paul Barker, the crown counsel lawyer at his office in Toronto.

Before Steven arrived back at the police station, he went to top up his gas tank for the next user of this vehicle. He then returned to the station and parked his car in the assigned spot. As he figured he was unlikely to go back out on the road, he took his duty bag inside the station with him. Once again sitting at a vacant desk he picked up the phone handset and placed the call to the Crown Counsel lawyer in Toronto. This time there was an answer.

The crown counsel lawyer seemed very pleasant over the phone. This was the first time Steven talked to Paul Barker, who was a long-time crown counsel lawyer in Toronto. Steven immediately felt comfortable talking to him, yet they were still both very professional over the phone. The crown lawyer instructed Steven that he should address him as Paul and that he wanted to know all about what Steven discovered starting from finding the dead lady a couple of weeks before and continuing right up to the present time. This information needed to include all the details of seeing the suspect at the funeral too. The crown lawyer, Paul, didn't seem at all surprised about the details of the romance scam crime. There was only one thing that surprised him and that was the fact that his main suspect in Toronto would show up to the funeral just to walk in and get the brochure of the service. There had to be a good reason for this, but what was it?

As the two of them talked on the phone, Steven provided his theory on why the thought this accused person would show up to this funeral all the way from Toronto. It wasn't until Steven told the crown counsel lawyer about the break-in at Janet's home and the computer, that is now at Stevens home, that Paul had made the connection that this must be exactly why the suspect person went there. Basically, the purpose of the trip was to steal the evidence that must be contained within the computer. It wasn't until he learned that this man came all the way from Toronto to Prince George that Steven realized how much of a trip this was and that there must be a piece of very good evidence located in the computer for Inegbedion to make this trip. He told Paul that he would double down on obtaining the data off her computer and would keep him up to date with any significant finding.

Chapter Six

About two weeks had passed by since Steven spoke to Paul with the Crown counsel office in Toronto. Steven was working diligently on the emails contained within Janet's computer any time he was off shift and had more than two hours free to attend to it. He was putting in considerable time into this task and he had completed reviewing about two thirds of the emails including the IP tracing and manually logging them all in the word file he created. He had produced nearly twenty-five pages of detailed notes for this chronological document he was creating. Each email was individually documented for the date and time it was received, the email IP address of where it was originally sent from, location of the sender as it was traced from the IP address, a brief note of its contents, and then any further note of importance. This was a long and exhaustive process, but one Steven hoped would pay off in the long run.

Steven was taking time to putting together an amazingly detailed chronology of what has transpired from the moment the two of them moved from the dating website and onto email; and it was through reading all her emails to the scammers that he felt like he really got to know Janet too. He learned about her personality and also her views and opinions on various topics. She was a far kinder and nicer person than he at first realized despite everyone telling him these things. The one thing that troubled Steven more than anything was that when he thought about how nice a person Janet was to others, and he learned more and more about how she was scammed, this brought a renewed sadness to him and she was too nice a lady to ever deserve this horrible treatment from these scammers. Not that anyone ever deserved to be their victims. But he knew that he could change his sadness into anger towards them, and further change that anger emotion into action.

On his next day at work, Steven received a message to call Paul Barker, the crown counsel in Toronto, at his earliest convenience. Once he had the opportunity, he headed back to the police station to place the call. He was put through to Paul and they spoke again.

"Steven, how are you doing my friend?"

"I am doing great. I am making considerable headway in the emails. It shouldn't be much longer, maybe one more month, and I will have this all done."

"You are not going to believe this one Steven. Last night the local police here in Toronto found a badly beaten corpse laying inside a dumpster in a back ally in a bad area of town. Without the medical examiners report the best guess currently is that the body likely had only been in there for a couple of hours prior to discovery. Positive identification has not yet been made but we are very sure it is Inegbedion."

"Wow, I didn't see that one coming. Do you know a motive for this?" Inquired Steven.

"Not yet, but we are all but certain that he was a member of Black Axe. Probably it is a result of him doing something very wrong and they killed him because of that. Or, it is possible that someone who was a victim of Black Axe did this to him, but we feel that this is not as likely as him being knocked off by his own group, especially based on the wounds he received and the extend of the beatings. But we do feel that he likely received the beating to death as a way to make examples of those that make mistakes. Sort of an encouragement to their other members not to screw up. They really are not a nice group."

"Why would Black Axe do this to one of their own members?" Inquired Steven.

"In addition to them being a criminal organization, they are also a cult based out of Africa. So, this member could have made an error in a criminal matter that exposed some of their members or he attempted to leave the group while knowing too much information about how they run and where they are all located. But I think it may be the first thing. You see, I have never heard of one of them showing up at the funeral of one of their victims in any country, ever. Let's not forget that this was a service where the member had to travel for many hours to attend at it. So obviously her death was a big deal to them for some reason. Therefore, I must think that this is likely related to the computer you have in your possession as you had suggested. I am betting that you will find a key piece of information on Janet's computer located somewhere in the files."

"When I talked to Janet's sister shortly after the death notification, she said I can keep the computer as long as I need it. I am about two-thirds finished logging all the emails, the IP addresses, and making notes of them in chronological order from the oldest email to most recent. There are so many of these emails, you have no idea. I have a word document that is now several pages long, and this is just the ones she has received. I still need to incorporate all her sent emails into the appropriate times and dates of my document. But sometimes when I need a break, I have read several that she has sent to them, but not all. I am so far concentrating only on the ones that the scammers had responded too or initiated. Also, she sent about two or three times more emails then she received. This was explained by the scammer as he can only get on the computer once or twice a day due to his work with the military. It seems like a good cover story if you ask me."

"It certainly does fit with the back story they created about the soldier. Any chance you can send me what you have now for the chronology, and later when you have completed it, you can send the full one to me?"

"I would be happy to do that for you, and of course when I am finished, I will send you the completed list too."

"I really appreciate it, and I appreciate all the hard work you are doing in this case. If I hear anything at this end that I think could assist you, I will let you know right away."

"And of course, I will do the same for you too."

"In the meantime, I will be attending court and asking for an abatement in his file once identification is confirmed and we have the death certificate. But if we have a motive based on your investigation, you never know, there may be a suspect arrested in the future for his death."

"Well, let us hope that the Toronto Police get a suspect, and I will see if I can find a motive."

"Maybe sometime in the future you will travel to the East and come to Toronto. Thank you for returning my call, Take care, Steven."

"It would be an honour to visit Toronto. I have always wanted to. Take care and bye for now."

With that Steven hung up the phone and decided to spend even more time outside of work hours getting these emails logged for Paul and the others investigating this crime. He also wondered what else he could do to get information to not only answer Janet's sisters' questions but also to help the officers in

Toronto in their investigation. Steven had felt a real sense of pride in this work that he had undertaken to complete. He originally hoped it would help in giving Marylin answers, and possibly even some closure on her sister's death. But the thought of gaining a conviction in a case in Toronto has pretty much ended as that person who he suspected as being the one convincing Janet to give her money away, is now dead. This change of circumstance had altered his focus and it was now to help others in the future avoid being victims of this devastating scam. But he did think to himself that it was still possible that he could find a reason for the murder in Ontario. He would certainly give it his best shot.

After work, Steven decided to sit down at the table for two hours of email searching. Just as before, as each email was read, the IP address would be checked and logged. Even with a renewed interest, this time he was feeling like it was quite tedious. Perhaps this was because Steven still had not found anything unique that would shine new light on this investigation. He was hoping for that key piece on information that would bust this case open. Finding the cornerstone email message that could open the doors to solving the murder was an idea that captivated Stevens attention. But he also knew it would be through his continued long hours of searching, reading, IP tracing and logging the information that show results only if he was lucky enough to even have that key piece of data to pass on.

Steven had never worked as a detective before, and he was still relatively new as a police officer. But he did enjoy doing this work even though it was very slow and laborious and feeling even slower each and every day. He knew that so much of this type of police work is slow, and he accepted this fact. Even routine patrols can sometimes seem like hours and hours of just driving around a neighbourhood, many night shifts were like this in the wee hours of the morning, but many took advantage of this time to finish off reports and to close off files.

But he also knew that it is the results that really matter most. He was reminded about one lesson he had while in police training in Regina. It is more important to lower the crime statistics in your patrol section than it is to get arrests. But both are good. Steven knew that with the main suspect dead, he is now searching for results to help stop this crime in the future. And he was determined to find these results. Sadly, not one person, or even one country would ever be able to stop this crime. But hopefully, he could save a few victims from future misery within his own country. At least this was his goal.

About two days later, Steven was nearing the end of reading and logging the details of all the incoming emails. There were less than ten left and then he would start to review all the outgoing emails sent by Janet to Benjamin. The very last email was in fact the first one he read, back when he first saw the computer at Janet's home, but then he started from the oldest and progressed in chronological order. Now that he was getting close to the end of all the incoming emails, he was wondering if all this work was all for nothing. There was so much to go through and read, as well as run the IP address, but so far all he learned was that Janet was essentially swindled out of a very large sum of money and left completely destitute by several people posing as just one person.

With only more six emails to go, Steven finally found it. Steven located the email that was the key to possibly unlocking this whole mystery. He must have stared at this email, reading it and then re-reading it at least a dozen times before he did anything else. Did this person really make this serious mistake? How could they be so careless as to allow this to happen? But Steven knew this was the corner piece in solving this whole puzzle. And now it may even lead to the motive of this group committing the ultimate crime; the crime of murder.

It seems that Inegbedion had accidentally sent Janet an email that was meant for his Black Axe bosses, and she was never supposed to learn about the contents. In this email, he talked about how they have just about bankrupt Janet and that there is likely nothing else he can get from her. He concluded that after Jideofor (a Nigerian name meaning 'you are justified') hacked into her financial situation with the bank, he thinks they should sever all contact and move on to find a new target as there was nothing more that they could get from her. This showed not only Steven, but anyone reading these emails, just how evil these people are, and how they do not care one bit about their victims, even after reading how nice she really is and they still want to hurt her this way and take every penny from her that they can. In Steven's mind this confirmed to him that these people are not even human, they are monsters who have no feelings or concerns for anyone else but themselves. They will drain their victims of their last cent, and they will only stop when there is nothing left to get from their victims. Steven was angry reading about their total disregard for others. It may have been wrong morally for Steven to feel this way, but he was not at all disappointed that Inegbedion got what he deserved.

When Janet received this unintentional email meant for someone else in the Black Axe organization, this naturally did not go over well with her. Reading her response email that she sent back had clearly indicated this fact to them. She likely knew she was swindled prior to this, but this received email had clearly confirmed it and this likely broke whatever was left of her spirit and her already badly damaged heart. She not only wrote of her contempt and displeasure to them, she stated that with this information, she was planning on passing this on to the police as she said to them that they could trace the email address back to them. To Steven, this was the proof that this group not only scammed Janet out of huge amounts of money, but the sender of the email also admitted that this group was responsible for hacking into either the bank or remotely into Janet's computer to see her finances. Now Steven would need to tell not only Robert with the RCMP Criminal Intelligence Program, but also Paul Barker the crown lawyer in Ontario and Detective Adrian Holland the detective in Toronto as it has a bearing on their files too. This email was likely the very cause of the trip to Prince George from Toronto. And now they all had it.

Unfortunately, tracing an email by the address is not actually that easy. Tracing it from the IP address is much easier, and Black Axe would certainly know this. They would also know that the IP address would be traceable to at least a geographical region, but not necessarily to an actual physical address. Also, there are ways to hide the IP address through the use of VPN's or 'virtual private network'. So, this posed the question to Steven, would the Black Axe person in Toronto need to relocate in order to have an IP address that would show a whole different geographical area? Did they bother to use a VPN? Steven didn't know the answer to this question, but he certainly knew who would likely know. Robert would certainly find this information useful, or at the very least, interesting.

At the next available opportunity, Steven called Robert to tell him of his discovery within the emails. Robert was happy to hear that Steven was getting good intelligence on this group. But the real case was not in

Prince George, the real case was in Ontario, specifically in Toronto. So, Steven called both Paul Barker and Detective Adrian Holland on a three-way conference call to advise them of this email he discovered.

"I bet you that Inegbedion was killed because after he accidentally sent that email, and then he flew to Prince George to retrieve the computer, containing the evidence that you now have, then he failed on this task, which now constitutes two major failures on his part. So, Black Axe sought their revenge on him. As it is a huge issue for them, they take these mistakes as a huge violation against Black Axe" said Detective Adrian Holland. "They have to punish the culprit and all the others in the organization must hear about it. So, they make him an example and let me tell you, the death was not quick and painless, far from it."

"I'll bet you are right, and it is a good theory for us to work off of anyway," replied Paul. "Perhaps Adrian, you should look into this theory more. Maybe see if there is anything else you have found that this ties into it. Great work Constable Browne, you must have worked very hard and I really appreciate it and all you have done. If you could please forward us both the email you found, plus your entire log file as I am thinking we will need it for the investigation and hopefully for a trial itself, that is if we discover who the perpetrator is and then have enough to make an arrest."

"I will send both of these documents to you right away" replied Steven.

With that, the call was ended, and Steven felt good about contributing meaningful information that may tie in with a murder investigation in Toronto. Never in his thoughts did he think that going to a simple break in call in a Summit Lake cabin could result in something this big.

So, the very next task was for him to forward this key email off to all that needed to see it, and in addition a copy of the log he created.

Naturally Steven needed to fill in his watch commander who was more than impressed at what had transpired. Steven knew this would help his career for when he would someday apply to other specialized sections within the RCMP.

Chapter Seven

For the next few months, the basic police work was continuing as normal with Steven. The routine was typical of this detachment's day to day incidents with only the occasional exception. His new friend Ed Scott had long ago left Summit Lake to return to his wife and his home in Surrey, British Columbia, but he would be coming back soon to enjoy the warmer summers and the longer hours of daylight. Steven stayed in contact with Ed, occasionally talking on the phone or by email. He knew that they would meet again, likely in a few weeks too. Steven would be certain to travel to the cabin to visit with him in about one month's time. This time Ed would be bringing his wife with him for some rest and relaxation at the lake. Steven said he would bring the scotch.

The weather was still on the cooler side, but it was very nice with the sun shining most days, and Steven was enjoying his time on the road as he was transitioning from being the rookie police officer, fresh out of Depot in Regina, to becoming a respected and valued member of the team in his detachment. He had proved himself with his peers and got the feeling that he was very liked by those who knew him. He was nearing the end of his day shift when he returned to the station to prepare to book off and head to visit his motley crew of friends.

Upon his arrival at the station, Steven was handed a letter from his watch commander, the letter came from the Ontario Crown Counsel office. Steven opened it and found a form inside commonly referred to as a 'LENS' which was an acronym for 'Law Enforcement Notification Sheet'. Basically, it was a law enforcement subpoena to attend court in Toronto as a witness in in a preliminary investigation in about two months' time.

This was a bit of a surprise for Steven as he was unaware that an arrest had even been made out East. It was a charge of first-degree murder whereby Abeo Adesina which ironically means 'one who brings happiness' was accused of murdering Inegbedion. Steven was aware who Inegbedion is, and that he was murdered and even more important, why he was murdered. But this was the first he ever heard of Abeo Adesina. It would be a preliminary inquiry prior to a trial at the supreme court level. This would be held in the Toronto Provincial Court and Steven would be required to travel there to give evidence on the emails and what he saw at the funeral. Basically, Steven had some of the evidence supporting the premeditation part of this murder.

Steven, standing next to his supervisor, showed him the forms right away as he had never been called to a court outside of Prince George, let alone one in a completely different province. Also, his court experience thus far has been exclusively traffic court. So, Steven received instructions from his supervisor on how members are to book their flights and hotels. He was advised to book plane tickets that are fully cancellable and last minute reschedulable. Often enough, witnesses are canceled at the last moment due to a guilty plea, or admission of certain evidence. Also, he could arrive at court on the specified time only to discover that he is not called to the witness stand that day, and he must come back to court the next day. So, he would need to re-schedule the return flight. For that reason, all flights for witness purposes are booked at the more expensive rate to be 100% cancellable.

With these instructions, Steven would book his tickets, but he would call Paul, the Crown Counsel lawyer, and Detective Adrian Holland, the Toronto Police detective the next morning first. Meanwhile, he would take an opportunity to put together the evidence as best he could so that it was presentable and easy to understand to the courts. In addition, he would take time to really learn all the details of his evidence as best as he could from memory.

The following morning Steven arrived at work and initiated a conference call with the Toronto Police officer and the Crown Counsel. The two of them on the phone together with Steven, were clearly reluctant to tell him too much that could influence his evidence, but they did advise him that based on Steven's discoveries, they determined the motive of the murder which is first, the accidental email and second, the failure to retrieve the computer and third to teach others what would happen if they failed with Black Axe. They could make the case of murder, but it is Steven's evidence that would show it to be first degree. It is believed that when this member of the Black Axe named Inegbedion made those two serious errors, the other member named Abeo, was sent to torture him to death as either a lesson to others not to make these kinds of mistakes or as a punishment for the errors he committed. Most likely it was for both reasons. Likely there were others involved in the murder, certainly whoever ordered it was also liable, but this was the one person they felt they has sufficient evidence to charge.

A couple of months had now passed since he received the notice to appear in court in Ontario to give the evidence, and Steven left for Toronto via Vancouver International Airport. He flew first into Vancouver one day early so that he could stop in at 'E' Division to meet with Robert from 'RCMP Criminal Intelligence Program' and hopefully have a good discussion about the group Black Axe as he clearly wanted to learn as much as he possibly could about them. It would be the first time the two of them actually met after so many phone calls. Robert seemed pleased to take the time to talk to Steven about this organization, Black Axe. In Robert's words, "It seemed that few people had even heard of them, let alone ones working in law enforcement." Robert was only too happy to share his knowledge with Steven on this notorious group. It was especially nice because he was imparting his knowledge on someone who was actually taking an active part in their prosecution and clearly wanted to know as much as he could about them.

"I must admit, prior to the discovery of Janet's body, and the subsequent investigation after that, I had never heard of Black Axe either," commented Steven. "Not until you told me about them. But hardly a day goes by where I am not thinking about them and wondering how I can learn even more. And perhaps it would be a good idea for this government to make more people aware of what they are doing."

"Unfortunately, there is just not enough information made public about this disgraceful group or other ones like them. Sure, many have heard about the Nigerian Prince scam. Everyone laughs at how stupid the scam is, but the simple fact is that many people still fall for it. Otherwise, they wouldn't waste their time doing it. But it is these romance scams that are believed to have nearly one thousand times more victims. I think the number may in fact actually be way higher."

"Why is that?"

"It goes back to my psychology days in university. Have you ever heard of Maslow's Hierarchy of Needs?"

"Yes, but it has been too long for me to clearly remember that lesson, I only vaguely recall it from my college days."

"The need for a person to feel love is right in the middle of the hierarchy, just above the need for the feeling of safety and right below the need for self esteem. These scammers focus on all three of those points. They cannot do much with the first level in the hierarchy, which is physiological. But if that is mostly there, and they focus on the next three, safety, love and esteem, then the top will be complete too. That one is self-actualization. They offer their victim the idea of safety in who they are as it is usually someone who is seen as a respectful or hero like person. The victim believed that through this person they had found their safety. As the next level is love and belonging, this is the main focus that the scammer does to their victim. The love the victims feel towards the scammer is very real, it just isn't reciprocated but the victim does not know that. Finally, the scammers work hard to build up the esteem of their targets, well at first anyway."

"What do you mean 'at first'?" asked Steven, clearly sensing that there is more to this statement than he at first heard.

"Well, they raise the victim's self-esteem to build them up and instill trust and build on their feeling of being loved. Then in time they will slowly and subtly lower their esteem to have the victim striving to impress the scammer to reacquire that feeling again. It is a very carefully laid out plan to essentially control this person. Think of it as a form of remove brainwashing, because this is really what it is. Of course, the victim will never quite get their esteem back to what it was before the requests for money comes in." Explained Robert. "and this is always done so subtly over time so that they never logically conclude that this is what is in fact happening to them".

"That explains another reason why these victims are willing to send them all their money. This is a very sad scam these people are pulling."

"Sadder than you could know. This group is responsible for taking millions of dollars each year from unsuspecting and vulnerable people. And that is just in Canada. They exist worldwide but no one knows how much money, precisely, they pull in through their scams. They have hurt so many lives and ruined many others too. The lucky victims only lose a couple of thousand dollars, but the unlucky ones lose everything. But the true numbers will never be known as it is believed that only about one percent of their victims report it to the police."

"Why is that?"

"Shame basically, combined with the sense that there is nothing that the police can do for them. Most victims feel very foolish for believing and trusting these scammers. So, they prefer to keep the details to themselves rather than report it. There is a fear of them being referred to as stupid and gullible, and not just by their friends and family, but by law enforcement too. So, the shame they feel is very strong and very real. But as you can see, it is a scam done over a long period of time by well-practiced scammers who are employing some very well practiced phycological controls on them."

"How does an organization like this work?"

"Well, there are a few different groups within the Black Axe organization with each doing different things or having different functions and specialties. So individually, one section on its own may not even be committing a crime in certain countries. Fortunately, in Canada, our laws are such that at the very least we can charge those ones with conspiracy to commit an offence. It is actually a very clever group and an ingenious scheme that they have put together. The first group of people targets dating sites and trolls for lonely people as their targets. Male or female, gay or straight, any race, it doesn't matter to them. In fact, the person that the targets are talking to are always male, with Black Axe anyway, but they could be posing as female, transgendered, gay, straight, or anything that attracts the other person. Once they have contacted their victim, they begin building positive dialogue and trust with their target. In time they suggest moving off the dating site and on to email. Again, this is to show trust to their victim as well as test and gain the trust of them too. Also, many dating websites look for signs of scammers and con-artists and may send an alert to the victim. This removes that problem for them at the same time as builds false trust. At that point the conversations are usually handed off to the next person in the organization. This next person can take a considerable amount of time taking the relationship further and priming them and setting them up for the eventual scam. They are well practiced smooth-talking people who build their victims self esteem and show them love. Their goal is to get their victim to fall in love with them in a big way, it goes back to the hierarchy we just discussed. When the relationship eventually gets to a certain point in perceived romance, love, and trust, the contact gets handed over to yet another next person who is better skilled at asking for and getting their target's money."

"This seems like so much work. But obviously it is effective;" commented Steven.

"It sure is, but now is where the real skills come into play. The progression must be very subtle for the scam to work. You see the first amount of money they ask for is tricky for the scammer to determine. They need to learn enough to know what the victim's assests are like. If they ask for too much too soon, then they quickly scare the target off. And if they ask for too little this will make it harder to get a good of amount of money later on. But they take their time to ask the right questions to ascertain the amount to ask. They are very skilled in determining these amounts. And the questions they ask seem so innocent that the information is given voluntarily most times. Sometimes a simple google search will reveal so much too. Like property values, civic taxes, amount of income based on their occupation. There really is so much information that they can use to determine the assets the person has. And let's not forget social media. A simple photo of a lady's garden can tell them so much. Or how about a photo of their new car. There really is so much information out there it is scary."

Robert continued on; "when it is established that money will in fact be sent, there is yet another player who comes into the story. This is a person who is frequently portraying a sibling or other trusted family member of the person asking for the money, or possibly some other cover story. They provide an account number through Western Union or other money transfer companies. Using a company like Western Union allows the scammer to use passwords instead of personal identification when they go to get the money sent to them."

"Western Union reminds me of how the Knights Templar created their banking system, using passwords and tokens." Commented Steven. "Well for a good purpose anyway."

"Yes, Western Union is a legitimate world-wide company, and the Templars were an honorable organization who in addition to setting up the first international banking system, also helped by keeping travelers safe from robbers and thieves. In this case, Western Union is doing their job, but Black Axe is abusing a legitimate service, and it is the Black Axe who are the robbers and thieves. I would even call these people monsters who use international financial organizations to assist in their scams on their victims. They do not care if they ruin other people's lives completely. They only care about how much money they can take from them."

"That is a very good point. But how do they make so much money based on how long it takes?"

"Their back story on what they are doing, like a soldier in a war-torn area, means they can only email once or twice a day. That is five minutes of work. They will likely be working on a couple hundred people at a time. So, it is a huge amount of cash coming in. But going back to the cash transfers, using the password they gave the victim, they would then go collect their gains from a Western Union or whatever money transfer service they use at that time. The member who collected the money would then deposit it into a bank account registered under a fake business name but really owned by the criminal organization. This money is all accounted for, and then the next group of people takes charge by assessing the amounts that each member has earned, and their 'pay' is distributed through the leadership of Black Axe. Those at the top of course taking the biggest cut and those at the bottom would take the smallest share. There are so many members behind the scene, such as hackers, and accountants, not to mention those that who are at the top of the pyramid within the cult. And make no mistake about it, this group is a cult. There is a religious component to them as well. That is why I do not hesitate in referring to them as a cult."

"Robert, I have to ask, I never understood about them being considered a cult. Can you tell me more about this please?" asked Steven.

"In this case it is a social group that is defined by its unusual philosophical beliefs, and by its interest in a common goal. They were at one time an idealistic university fraternity. But that was a very long time ago. Since then the group has morphed into what it is today. And they have been linked to decades of murders and rapes, and its members are said to swear a blood oath. Also, cult activities are secretive. We have limited information on their rituals, oaths of secrecy, and their use of symbols or peculiar signs. The religious component is still to be completely learned, but we do know it exists. They are referred to as a 'death cult' back in Nigeria too.

"That sounds like a cult to me." Replied Steven.

Chapter Eight

Early the very next morning Steven woke up and checked out of the hotel he was staying at in Vancouver. He traveled by taxi to the Vancouver Airport Domestic Gate to check-in and catch his flight to Toronto. After the usual screening and wait time, he boarded the plane and was on his way to Toronto's Pearson International Airport. It was a policy that RCMP officers requiring longer flights, would fly in business class. So, Steven was quite comfortable on this flight. Even the meals were better here, as well as the portions were larger too. It was his first-time flying business class and he quickly learned that this was a nice, albeit expensive way to travel. Also, with him being a little on the taller side, the extra leg room was very appreciated.

After about four and a half hours, Steven's flight arrived at Pearson International Airport and he caught another taxi to a nice hotel that was still a reasonable distance from the courthouse in Toronto. Typically, in most cities, you need to be a little farther away from the courthouse to be in a better area. So, using this advice, Steven selected one with decent online review, he was also happy to learn that his hotel had a gym in it too.

After checking in to his room, he dropped his bags on the bed and opened the blinds to have a good look out the window from the high up floor his suite was on. As this was Stevens first time in Toronto, he was hoping to have a nice view of the CN tower, but sadly he could not see it from his window. Of course, he didn't even know what direction it was in, but at least he still had a very nice view. He unpacked his luggage into the furniture in his room and decided to leave his room to find somewhere to have either an early dinner or a late lunch. But going through the restaurant lobby in the hotel, he spotted their in-house restaurant and he thought it looked pretty good to him, so that is where he decided to eat his early dinner.

After finishing his meal, Steven thought it would be nice to take a long walk to explore the neighbourhood of Toronto that his hotel was located in. He knew that the hotel was considered a nice one, and looking around the neighbourhood, he could sense that it was probably a reasonably good area of town with just an average amount of crime. He understood all major cities have crime, and especially near hotels were the tourist are. Even though he was very observant of his surroundings, he saw no one who stood out as a concern for his safety or security.

After his long walk exploring this neighbourhood in Toronto, Steven went back to the hotel and his room and watched TV for some time as he had nowhere else to be, and little else to do. But this quickly became boring for him so he went to the hotel's gym for a workout and proceeded to exercise for some time until it became late enough that he would be able to get a good night's sleep. As he was working on British Columbia time, and he was presently in Ontario, the three hours difference made it a little hard to get to sleep at a reasonable time, so he watched TV again, while in bed, for about two more hours. Finally, he was able to get to sleep, albeit very late in Ontario time.

The next morning, Steven woke up at an hour that seemed way too early for him due to the different time zone variances. After his routine morning ablutions, he then went to the same hotel restaurant again for a large breakfast before catching a taxi to get to the courthouse. Once out of the taxi, he entered the court building and went through the security screening entrance. For a moment he thought of showing his badge to bypass the security, but as he was not armed, he decided to simply put the contents of his pockets into the tray and proceed through. The officer opened his wallet and saw the badge and quickly closed it and handed it back to him before he walked through the metal detector. Naturally it went off, but the second officer saw him being handed his items before he walked through so he was not stopped. He was now wondering if he should have shown his badge when he arrived. But as the security staff made no mention of anything after discovering his badge, he thought that they likely assumed him to be undercover and didn't want to draw attention to him. So, they simply waved him through the screening station. Also, they never asked him if he was armed. Next time, Steven would just show his badge, armed or not.

He approached the information counter and asked the staff there where he could find the crown counsel office and specifically Paul Barker. Once provided with the directions, he made his way to that floor to see Paul at his office where the two of them would talk and go over his evidence prior to court. It was at this meeting that Steven learned that Abeo was out of custody and on bail. Steven was certain that the bail amount must have been set high to prevent him from running and leaving Canada. But in addition to that, his passport was likely surrendered to the court too. The conversation lasted for about half an hour before the two of them left to go to the courtroom for the start of the second day of the preliminary inquiry.

Steven had to wait on the hard bench seats in the court hallway until he would be called to the witness stand for giving his evidence to the judge hearing the preliminary inquiry. He only had to wait about fifteen minutes before he was called to the witness box. He was the first witness that day on the inquiry. Once on the stand, he took the bible in his hand and was sworn in and the direct examination by the crown began.

Steven explained how some time ago he took a call to the north of Prince George to Summit Lake British Columbia to attend a break and enter call at a wilderness cabin. He explained about the note found inside the cabin and how the trail of footsteps in the snow led to finding a dead lady. He explained to the court about how he learned of her financial troubles through her sister and how the bank could not confirm it, but the supreme court in Prince George did have a foreclosure file opened for the victims' home. He handed over a copy of the 'Notice of Civil Claim' from the Supreme Court of British Columbia that was given to him by the court registry in the court back in Prince George. This became an exhibit in the preliminary hearing.

Next, Steven explained how he had received permission from Janet's sister to take the computer from Janet's home. He had the computer back at his home and spent almost six weeks documenting the emails and he produced the multi-page word document listing what he had found. This too became exhibit six for the court.

Finally, Steven produced the email that was sent to Janet in error. This was a key piece of evidence towards motive. This also became an exhibit of the preliminary inquiry.

While on the witness stand Steven talked about going to Janet's funeral and seeing a black male who was out of place and caused Steven to pay attention to him. He gave details about leaving the building to see where he went.

Paul Barker asked; "if the clerk could please hand the witness exhibit two of the preliminary inquiry?"

The clerk of the court handed Steven a small Cerlox bound binder that contained only about fifteen double sided pages. Inside this binder were several colour photographs with two pictures per page. The first two pages showed color pictures of Inegbedion. One appeared to be a police photograph upon his arrest, showing both a front and a side view of his head. The next five pages contained crime scene pictures of Inegbedion now clearly dead. There were crime scene photos showing where the body was found, and the clothing worn by him. The final pages contained autopsy pictures of Inegbedion clearly placed on a medical examiner's table undergoing dissection for the autopsy.

"Constable Browne, you had a moment to look through these pictures. Do you recognize the person depicted in the photos contained within this exhibit?"

"Yes, this is the person I saw attending the funeral."

"Thank you. Did anything else happen during the time of this funeral?"

"I didn't know at the time, but I later learned through a police report that within an hour either side of when I saw Inegbedion at the funeral, Janet Boyd's house was broken into."

"When did you learn about the break-in?"

"When I first arrived at work following my days off. The file created by the officer attending the break-in was linked to my file electronically and the file created when Janet was reported as missing."

"When you learned about the break-in at her home, what did you do?"

"I retrieved the police report from the computer, and I reviewed it. The report indicated that the only thing that appeared missing was the computer. That was the same computer I had taken with the permission of the victim's sister Marylin. So, I made a note to this file indicating that I was in possession of it."

"And then?"

"I decided to go talk to the neighbours in the immediate area and see if there were any possible witnesses. One neighbour told me of seeing a man about the same age as Inegbedion and matching the same description, including the clothing, of the person I saw at the funeral. The time frame given to me by this witness was about an hour either side of when I saw him."

"Did you do anything further after learning about this?" asked Paul Barker.

"Yes, I formed the opinion that Inegbedion had likely been the person who broke into Janet's home with the intent on taking the computer to prevent law enforcement from finding the email, that is now an exhibit, which was accidentally sent to her."

"That opinion was based on the email that you showed the court as exhibit seven?"

"That is correct."

"Based on this, did you form an opinion on why Inegbedion was murdered?"

"Objection your honour" stated the defense counsel. "This calls for speculation on the part of Constable Browne;" spoke the defense counsel.

"Your honour this is a case where it is the very speculation that pointed him in the direction of the purpose of this investigation. I agree it is speculation on the part of constable Browne, and although it is speculation, at this point, it is where the evidence led and therefore where the investigation went," commented Paul to the Provincial Court Judge hearing the preliminary inquiry.

After some talk between the defence counsel and the judge, the objection was overruled, and Steven was permitted to answer the question.

"Going back to the question, I had to assume that Inegbedion was murdered because of accidentally sending Janet the incriminating email that was meant for his superiors, and secondly because of his failure to retrieve the computer containing this email."

"Thank you, Constable Browne," turning towards the judge, Paul Barker said; "I have no further questions for this witness."

At this point the defense counsel stood up and stated; "defence has no questions for this witness." This is not unusual for the defence not to ask questions at a preliminary hearing. Often, they leave their biggest defence questions and theories for the actual trial. So, with this, Steven left the witness stand and took a seat in the court gallery with the intent of watching the remainder of the preliminary inquiry to hear the results. Nearly all of them proceed to trial, and this one would likely be no different.

Around noon, the court took the lunch break and both Paul and Steven went for lunch at a nearby restaurant.

"You did very well on the stand. Your evidence showed confidence and the facts showed through. I anticipate you will be back here in about one year to give evidence at his trial. Unless his lawyer feels that a guilty plea would be better. But I have no idea what they plan to do at the actual trial itself."

"Other than traffic court, this is actually my first-time giving evidence."

"Well, you did a great job."

"Good to hear as I have some other court dates coming up in the next few months. Nothing as big as this though."

"I have to get back early to prepare for closing. I got the bill, and I will see you back at the courtroom."

"Sounds good, I will see you there."

With this, Paul left the restaurant and shortly after Steven made his way back to the courthouse. Once again after clearing the security gate, this time showing his badge to the staff at the gate, he proceeded back to the courtroom that was hearing this preliminary inquiry. When the court went back in session, Paul gave his closing remarks as did the defence counsel, although his were very limited in content. The judge waisted no time in giving his ruling on this hearing. As it was not a trial, they do not have to go into great detail outlining the evidence, or the reason for their decision, and that is pretty much the way it went. The judge simply announced that he sees a reasonable chance for a conviction on this matter, therefore this case will be transferred to the Superior Court of Ontario for the purpose of a trial. Then a next appearance date was given to the accused and his lawyer on the spot for a fix-date hearing at the higher court. It was about one month away for the fix-date to occur.

With that decision out of the way, the court was now adjourned for the day. Steven said goodbye to

Paul, and he made his way down to the main floor and out of the building and out to the street.

Steven exited the building and stood there for a moment watching as Abeo walked past him. It was there that he noticed as Abeo gave Steven a dirty look over his shoulder. Steven was reasonably certain that he also heard Abeo Adesina call him an asshole in a quiet, almost inaudible voice, but rather than be upset by that comment, Steven had to suppress a burst of laughter at Abeo's pathetic attempt at an insult aimed at him. All that Abeo managed to succeed with this comment was to convince Steven that his evidence was accurate and well delivered. This reinforced his belief that there would be a conviction in in the future.

Just as Abeo got about twenty feet away, Steven suddenly and without any warning heard a loud 'crack'. Then a fraction of a second later and just behind him, over his right shoulder, there was something that appeared like a puff of smoke from the concrete wall of the courthouse building. It took only a very brief moment for him to realize that the crack sound was a bullet flying right past his head and striking the concrete wall only a few feet behind him. The smoke was in fact dust from the bullet striking the concrete wall after the bullet flew past his head before ricocheting on the concrete behind him. Steven later realized that this bullet had likely traveled level to his head and mere inches from striking him right in his face. Almost instantly his reflexes kicked in and Steven ran about fifteen feet and hit the ground very fast behind a concrete embankment and shuffled back behind the abutment to protect himself from the next shot that he was waiting for to come. He yelled at others to immediately take cover, which some did, and some just ran away. Fortunately for everyone around him, there were no further shots, just that one that nearly hit him. He immediately felt the adrenalin surge through him as his heartrate nearly instantly tripled and his breathing became deep. His first thought after gaining cover was that he really wished he had his side arm now. He had even instinctively reached for his non-existent holster.

His next thought was to protect the public around him. He looked to ensure that everyone was physically safe and behind some sort of cover. A quick scan from over the concrete cover showed that everyone was safe and in a good position, so Steven quickly lowered his head behind the cover before a second shot could come. Fortunately, there were no further shots fired.

The court security didn't come out like Steven thought they would, but he was certain that they were observing as safely as they possibly could. His heart was racing. The adrenaline was causing him to shake, but instead of being scared, he was hyper-alert to all that was going on around him. He thought to himself, 'if I had to shoot back, I couldn't hold my pistol steady'. Of course, he was unarmed as all his duty equipment is back in British Columbia.

People were now running away, and there were others who hit the ground out in front of the courthouse. Steven yelled at them to stay behind the same concrete barrier that he was currently behind. He noticed a couple of people lying flat on the ground and he told them to move behind the concrete with him. Laying there simply made the others a much better target to whoever was shooting. Steven even considered running back into the courthouse, but he quickly dismissed the idea when he thought about the cover he had behind the concrete. It was good cover and there was no sign of anyone approaching the court building, so his best option was to stay right where he was. Besides, the court security staff were probably watching for an active shooter in the area and formulating a plan. As much as he wanted them out there to assist, he knew from his training that they were formulating a plan rather that just running outside and possibly into a shooter's sights. He also knew that the Toronto Police were likely in the surrounding area doing a sweep to ensure the public's safety.

All the lessons that Steven learned about active shooters were coming back in his mind. 'Run-Hide-Fight' was the message that came back to him. When you are unarmed and a target, your first priority is to create distance between you and the shooter. If you cannot run, you should hide. In this case, Steven hid behind a concrete wall for safety. The last step is to fight, but this was the last thing that you should attempt. Steven looked around him to see what he could use as a weapon if needed to go to the last option. He did see a heavy concrete ashtray for the smokers to use. It looked very heavy to wield around, but if needed he could use it as a weapon. He was so alert to everything going on around him that he even noticed that there was a sign on the wall next to the ashtray stating that you cannot smoke within five meters of the door, yet he was certain that the ashtray was only about three meters from the door. He couldn't help but wonder why he noticed such things when he was facing the possibility of being shot. He almost laughed about this but re-focused on all that was going on around him.

What seemed like almost an hour later but was in fact just under ten minutes since the shot was fired, the Toronto Police were filling the area and indicating it was now safe. They ushered all the possible witnesses back into the lobby of the courthouse to get statements from them. Steven was now back in the lobby of the court building giving his statement to one of the police officers and to one of the court security members at the same time.

Steven thought it was likely the police had actually arrived in the vicinity much sooner then he saw them, but they needed to clear the area to ensure there would be no more shots and the safety of the public and the attending officers was always a priority. There was just the one Toronto police officer interviewing Steven while others were scouring the area looking for a shooter, or any signs of one. This did not include the court security officer who was also taking detailed notes.

Steven was surprised to learn that the Toronto Police did locate a witness of the gunman. He was a homeless man who was pushing his shopping cart full of his dumpster treasures retrieved through his recycling work. He was giving the police a description of the suspect and he advised the police of what he saw. He described the shooter as a 'black man but without dreadlocks, and very dark skin firing a hunting style rifle with a big scope mounted on it. He was pointing it out of his car window.' The description of a black man without dreadlocks was likely a reference to the larger Jamaican population in the greater Toronto area.

This man went on to say that the shooter had only taken one shot and then withdrew the rifle back through the driver's window and he calmly drove away from the area. Based on the information that the homeless man gave the interviewing officer, it was suggested it was likely not a Jamaican man, who are quite common in Toronto, but perhaps an African man who fired the rifle. Unfortunately, that man was a little stunned at what he saw, and not very familiar with different vehicles. All they could get from this man by way of a description is that it was a dark blue sedan. He didn't even get a partial plate number. But at least the police now knew that the area was likely safe for the time being, and that the shooter was using a long gun.

Paul Barker had previously come down from his office after learning that it was now safe to do so. Of course, once he learned that Steven was the target, he became very concerned for him. After learning that Steven was fine, he had suggested to the Toronto Police that it was possible that there was no intent to kill or even harm Steven. It was possible that this was simply a message for Steven not to give evidence at the future trial of Abeo. Of course, this also makes Paul a target on this matter too, and this caused considerable concern for all involved. After all, Paul was the crown lawyer who was prosecuting this matter. Paul would be talking to his employer about the safety of himself and perhaps raising the level of this trial's security. But that would be the call of the court security and police.

It was during the interview with Toronto police and the court security that Steven noticed that the adrenaline surge that he was experiencing was now beginning to subside. Steven was now detecting the exhaustion and the excessive perspiration that this rush leaves behind. Paul obviously sensed that and invited him back to his office for a beverage from the staff refrigerator. But the police wanted to continue talking to Steven, so Paul went on his own to bring him back a can of coke. Steven consumed the coke very quickly and thought that this beverage never tasted better than it did now.

Steven requested the file number from the Toronto police officer as he knew he would likely need to file his own report once he arrived back home in Prince George. Maybe he would see if he could pick up a pad of paper from the hotel so he could write down the details during his flights home. They he would only need to type it in at his police station, or even from the patrol car.

After Steven's interview with the Toronto Police was concluded, one of the police officers offered to give Steven a ride back to his hotel, calling it a professional courtesy extended to a fellow police officer. Steven was looking forward to getting out of his now sweaty suit and go hit the hotel's gym to help reduce some stress. After that he would have a nice long and hot shower to help settle himself down. Although tired from the adrenalin surge, he new the exercise would be good for him. After today's events, he felt he could really use a good workout, even if it would end up being a shorter one then usual.

The Toronto police officer dropped Steven off at his hotel and he went first to his room to change into workout clothing and then off to the hotel's gym. He started out doing a cardio workout, but he was having a harder time then he normally should. He was spending about half an hour on the exercise bike with the tension set higher that he normally would so that it would tire him out more quickly. Even with the tension set higher, he clearly felt that the events in the afternoon made him more tired than he at first realized he was. He had to turn the tension down on the stationary bike after a few minutes. This was followed by spending some time on the universal weights machine. He even had to reduce the weights from his normal routine. This was likely all to do with the body's normal reaction to an extreme fight-or-flight situation, and not a reflection of his own physical abilities. Finally, after a shorter than normal, but still good work out, he made his way back to the hotel room and discovered that the phone had a message light blinking on it, indicating he had a call in his absence. Retrieving the message, he heard Paul ask to call him. Nothing urgent just wanting to know if he was available for dinner.

Steven didn't want to miss Paul before he left from work, so right away he phoned Paul on his cell phone number that was provided in the message. Paul must have had call display on his phone and recognised the hotel name because he answered indicating that he knew it was Steven on the other end.

"Steven, you have traveled east a long way to visit here. Perhaps we can have dinner tonight, that is if you haven't already eaten?"

"Dinner sounds like a fantastic idea. But I just returned from the gym and desperately need a shower first."

"No worries, I will pick you up in half an hour if that is enough time. Look for a black Chrysler 300 SRT sedan out in front of the hotel."

With that, Steven hung up the phone and attended to his personal ablutions prior to going out for dinner. A short time later, Steven was waiting just inside the hotel door looking for Paul's car to pull up out front. Almost to the minute, Paul's vehicle arrived at the curb. Steven exited the hotel and joined Paul in his car.

"How would you like to have Pizza for dinner?" asked Paul.

"Who doesn't love a good pizza?" replied Steven, without any hesitation.

"Fantastic, there is a nice pub a few blocks away, and they have really nice food there to. They even cook their pizzas in a brick oven too."

Before long the two of them reached the pub. They exited the car and entered the pub where they took a seat just far enough away from others so that they could talk without being easily overheard. They both ordered beverages. Steven liked a good beer, but Paul was more of a wine drinker. With ordering their food and beverages out of the way, they continued their conversation first started in the car.

"So, I wanted to tell you I was very impressed to hear that someone as recently out of Depot as you were when you started on this investigation, persevered and uncovered such a big case. Most constables would never do the level of work you did, and your documentation was impeccable."

"Thank you, that is a huge big compliment for me. I really enjoyed doing that, and creating the document showed me clearly how this whole process unfolded. I feel like I had learned so much from this task."

"Well, the work you did on this case turned out to be so important in learning the motive. I think there is a great chance we will get a conviction partly because of what you put together, combined with the work of Toronto Police. But it was you who put forward the motive that Toronto PD could not figure out."

"Thank you, I appreciated that. And honestly, I learned so much from this experience. I hope it will help to make me a better police officer as I advance in my career."

"Listen Steven, I wanted too talk to you about that. I was talking to some guys I know in the Special I section. There may be an opening coming up in a few months time in Ottawa. I think you should seriously consider applying. And if you do, I would be happy to write a reference letter for you."

"I have thought about what I want to do with the RCMP, but I haven't decided what area I wanted to go in. But I must admit I felt a real sense of accomplishment on this entire case and I can see myself enjoying doing this work on an ongoing basis. Perhaps I will give Special I some serious consideration."

"Great. I think you should start working on your cover letter and your curriculum vitae. Always keep it up to date as new certificates, courses, and experiences come up. Even if you do not go into Special I, you never know when you will need to produce it. Maybe you will need it for court, or maybe for a job application. But you should always keep it current."

"Funny you say that, my watch commander recently told me to update my CV as well because I have just about completed my one year of the field training component of my policing career. I suspect I will be transferred a way from Prince George soon anyway. I was thinking of applying to the lower mainland near Vancouver, but now you have me thinking of maybe this opportunity here in Ontario."

"Well honestly Steven, how many constables are there who this early on in their career take a seemingly simple break and enter case and through extreme diligence, track it back to a major international crime ring? I will tell you the answer; very few my brother, very few. I personally have never heard of it happening before. Most constables would have finished off the suicide report and called it a day; that is it. You were diligent and followed a hunch, or curiosity. Look how far that hunch took you. Okay, so many hunches do not work out this way, but that is what police work is all about, and you also showed resourcefulness in obtaining the evidence too."

"My watch commander said the same thing to me a few months ago. Okay, you have me convinced, I will apply to Special I when the position becomes available. You have twisted my rubber arm."

"Great, another thing I also wanted to talk to you about is that I really believe that the incident at the courthouse this afternoon was likely just a warning to you, and you are probably perfectly safe until the actual trial date. That is how Black Axe works, they like to intimidate people. I want to ensure you that when the trial comes, there will be extra protection methods employed. You will not be coming in through the front door at the courthouse, nor will you be on the street anywhere near the building. You will have a security escort both ways to and from the hotel. In fact, the hotel will not even be booked under your name, but under an alias."

"Thank you. Prior to the incident today I have never been shot at before. I hope it is the last time too. I must admit, at first my reactions kicked in, more than my actual thoughts on what was happening, but once I realized it, well let's just say I am surprised my shorts stayed clean."

"No kidding. I think I would have the same issue. Also, it was on the evening news, but the media reported it as a street gang shooting trying to take out a rival member. They even said that the person missed. We of course believe it was on purpose that they missed. And as for the gang shooting, let's leave them thinking just that."

"Considering that the homeless witness said there was a big scope on the rifle, I am inclined to agree with you about it being an intentional miss. Of course, it could be that the sites were just way off, or he is a lousy shot."

"I disagree. The Black Axe knows that if they killed you, the wrath they faced from law enforcement throughout North America would make their work so much harder. So, they send a message that will prompt an investigation that will likely provide no leads. No member of Black Axe, or anyone affiliated with them will talk at all. They are way to scared to do that as they know that they will be the next victim and that their death will not be quick and painless. That is how they work."

"Based on that, I have to fully agree with you, the shooter missed hitting me on purpose," replied Steven. "I guess in a strange way, his shot wasn't a miss at all."

"Good point."

The two of them enjoyed their festive time together over their individual pizzas, wine and beers. The conversation was good, and Steven felt he now had a good friend even though they lived in different provinces an had only recently met. Unfortunately like all good social times, they were happy to meet and sorry to part. And all too soon it was time to call it a night and Paul gave him a drive back to his hotel.

It was very early the next morning when Steven woke up and caught a taxi back to Pearson International Airport for his return flight back to Vancouver and then transfer on to Prince George. He was still on British Columbia time, so it seemed so much earlier to him when he awoke. He waited until he cleared security before he purchased some breakfast for himself at one of the fast food kiosks at the airport. He brought the meal and coffee with him and sat down at his gate and had his breakfast right there. After he finished, including his first coffee, he then waited for his plane to start loading. Fortunately, it wasn't too long before the airline was calling for business class passengers to board the plane. Once again, he had a nice comfortable seat in the business class section.

Even before the regular passengers started boarding, the flight attendant in business class asked Steven if he would like a newspaper to read. Of course, he said yes as it would be a long flight back. She handed him a copy of the Toronto Sun paper and he began to read it. He did see one story that caught his attention; on the second page there was an article about how someone took a shot at a gang member outside of the courthouse and then sped away. Steven had a hard time not laughing out loud as he never thought he would be considered a 'gang member'. The newspaper also showed in another unrelated story to that shooting but also within same section of the paper, the author talked about a murder preliminary inquiry hearing that will now be sent up to supreme court for a full trial. Due to a ban on publication there was not much else that the newspaper could report, but there was enough information within this article for Steven to know that this was the case he was in Toronto giving evidence on.

After he finished reading the newspaper, Steven decided to keep the article for the novelty of being referred to as a gang member. He then removed from his bag a pad of paper to start writing the details of his 'incident' outside of the Toronto courthouse. He thought about this and concluded that it would likely be viewed as an on-duty shooting as he was attending as a police officer. He attempted to note all the details he could recall, fortunately he also had the Toronto Police file number to place in his final report. It took him about an hour to recall all the details he felt necessary for the report he would need to write. It had been an interesting two nights and one full day in Toronto. It was certainly a business trip he was not soon to forget.

Other than the notes and the newspaper, the flight back to Vancouver as well as the transfer to a second flight on to Prince George was pretty much unremarkable and routine. He did have a lunch on the flight into Vancouver, but after he departed that plane and waited for the next one to Prince George, he found he had a two hour lay over so he took advantage of the airports restaurants and had a better sit down meal that left him feeling a little more satisfied than the airplane snack sized lunch. He then went back through security and boarded his final plane on to Prince George. A few hours later he was back home and preparing for what would be the second shift of his two-night shifts before having his next four days off.

After Steven arrived back at his home he decided to try and stay up late as well as sleep in longer so that his night shift the following evening will go smoothly. He thought about calling Marylin to tell her about the preliminary hearing but decided against it as he would wait until he was back on his normal shift and on duty.

He did make himself a late dinner to keep himself occupied to stay up late. With dinner now on his plate, he sat down to watch the late news, the national news of Canada. He was not surprised, yet still a little bit disappointed not to see anything on the late news about the case he was working on. It may be a good local story in Toronto, but it was not likely to be considered important enough to make the national news all the way on the west coast. Still, Steven held on to the newspaper from Toronto. He wondered if he should make a scrap book of newspaper clippings detailing his career.

Chapter Nine

The next night Steven returned to work to begin the last of his two consecutive night shifts. As he was away the previous three days, he spent a little longer than usual reading the statistics on what is happening in his patrol area as well as any alerts that he needed to be made aware of. There was the usual number of break ins, vandalism, and graffiti, along with the ever-present domestic assault calls and shoplifting reports, theft of and theft from automobiles. There was nothing that alerted him to any special types of crime, just the usual and routine calls. So, it wasn't long before he went out on the road to begin his shift and heading into his patrol area.

Before commencing his patrols, Steven's shift supervisor called him into the office as he had previously learned about the shooting in Toronto. Steven was told about the services available to members who experienced these situations. Critical incident Stress or CIS was always a concern, as is Post Traumatic Stress Disorder, or PTSD. Steven was handed a card with a phone number he could call if he felt he could use the employee assistance program. After a few minutes of talking to his watch commander about the events in Toronto, he left to resume his usual patrols.

While Steven was out on the road, he decided to drive by Marylin's home and see if she was there. He wanted to tell her all that has happened over the past few months. He went to her home and knocked on her door, she was home and invited him inside. She was clearly happy to see him after several months of no new news. The last time they talked was back when he came by to return Janet's computer to her some time before. Once there at her home, he began to tell her all that has transpired, including his recent trip to Toronto. She was happy to hear that there was something happening against this group, even if it was not specifically about Janet. There was even a look of happiness learning that the very person believed to be the one corresponding to Janet was now their own victim. Steven omitted the details about how they torture them to death to make an example to the others.

When Marylin learned that Steven was even shot at while in Toronto, not only did she gasp in shock, Steven could tell that she had to fight her own tears. He had assured her that it was nothing more than a dramatic scare tactic aimed at stopping him from attending the trial when it eventually happens. He also told her that when the trial does eventually happen, he will be very well protected by the Toronto Police. So, she had nothing to worry about for him. Still it showed the kind of family that Marylin and Janet had come from. She was very concerned for others, and from what Steven knew of Janet, she was very much like that too. That fact reinforced in his mind why he would do all this work.

After about half an hour of his visit with her, he decided it would be best to get back on the road and do some work. There were no calls pending in his area, which on its own was very unusual at this time of the early evening. So, he decided to set up to catch some speeders on a street notorious for people driving too fast. Steven enjoyed doing traffic stops and learned from a senior member that he should always treat traffic court seriously.

"You never want to make a mistake giving evidence in a supreme court; therefore, you should always treat traffic court as the highest court in the land." This senior officer would go on to tell him; "If your evidence is good at the traffic court level, it will likely be good at the supreme court level too, but if your evidence is bad at traffic court, it will be consistently bad no matter what the level of court you are attending."

This advise made sense to Steven, and he took that guidance seriously and especially now that he will be returning to Ontario to the Superior Court sometime in the future. He knew that his evidence must be perfect when he goes back there for court, especially if he wants to see a member of Black Axe convicted for their heinous crimes. Any potential flaw in his testimony will result in defence counsel exploiting it to the point where all his evidence might become suspect to the courts.

When Steven wrote up a ticket, he made sure to always take the time to write down any notations that would assist him if the ticket was to be disputed. His notes were meticulous, which was a skill that would end up serving him well in his future with the RCMP, especially if he ever got into the Special I section as he was now considering. So, it was with that in mind that Steven made a conscious effort to maintain better notes, not just on major incidents, or violation tickets, but to be in the habit of drafting meticulous notes and reports on everything. But it was also important to be very factual. If he didn't know something it was better to state that. It was far better to lose a case because you don't know something then it was to be misleading. He knew that once you lose your credibility, it is near impossible to ever get it back. And to Steven, his integrity meant everything to him.

It was now getting close to the end of his shift, and the end of the four-day rotation that he had only worked one day on due to his court attendance in Ontario. It was at this time that he got a message on his mobile computer to phone Paul Barker with the Ontario Crown Counsel office in Toronto. So, he drove straight back to the police station and placed the call to him. He now had the direct number for Paul's desk, so he didn't go through the receptionist or the after-hours automated tree.

"Hi Paul, Steven here. How are you doing?"

"Steven, good to hear from you. I am fine. It has been how long? Oh yes, almost three whole days, (the two laughed over this point). I thought you might find this news interesting. It seems that Abeo Adesina never reported to his bail supervisor as he was required to do. He was supposed to be there first thing in the morning after the preliminary inquiry. So, the bail supervisor tried repeatedly to call him or anyone who would know his whereabouts. The Toronto Police were sent to his residence, and it appears that he has vacated the address. He basically disappeared. So, with that, a Canada wide warrant has been issued for his arrest."

"Interesting. I wonder where he is now. Are the local police there looking into his disappearance?"

"Yes, but not the Toronto Police Department, this has been handed over to the RCMP here in Ontario."

"Why not the Toronto Police or the OPP?" (Ontario Provincial Police)

"Well, believe it or not, we think he may have left Ontario."

"Wasn't there a high bail set for his release?"

"Yes, but maybe he had far more money that we had thought he had, either that or the Black Axe funded it because he is far higher in the organization than we had thought he was. What we do know for sure is that he violated his bail conditions by failing to report, and then there is his disappearing."

Steven then joked "I hope he isn't coming to Prince George anytime soon."

With that said, the two exchanged some pleasantries before disconnecting from the call. Paul assured Steven that if there is any further news, he would pass it on to him right away.

With this information, Steven booked off for the shift and began the start of his days off until the whole rotation started all over again.

During his days off, Steven hung out with his friends and made it to the Friday night dinner at the family owned restaurant. One of the men from the group would be moving the next day into a new house, so he was not there that evening. But they all planned to assist in the move the following day to make the work much lighter for him. They figured with about twenty men, four or five pick-up trucks, and this is not including the wives of some of these men, they figured they can have him out of his old house and into the new one in less than three hours. The wives would be packing and unpacking as well as cleaning the new place and also cleaning up the old. In addition, some of them would be taking care of lunch and possibly dinner too. Steven knew that no matter where he would end up living, he had family in Prince George that would be there for life.

A few days after that Steven returned back to work to start the first of his two repeated day shifts that precede the two consecutive night shifts. While there at the police station, he received a call from the RCMP Criminal Intelligence Program in Toronto and Robert from RCMP Criminal Intelligence Program in the greater Vancouver office was also on the phone as a conference call. It seems that the Criminal Intelligence section in Toronto had intel that Abeo Adesina likely fled Canada, probably he was on route to Nigeria at that exact time.

"Even without his passport?" Asked Steven.

"Simple, we believe that he was placed on a freighter that is heading straight from Halifax to a west African coastal country before finally stopping at Lagos, Nigeria where he will likely disembark. Black Axe has the money to move him out and they have the power and control back in Nigeria to bring him in without any documentation. Sorry to tell you this, but he will most likely never be back to face this murder charge here in Canada. And as he likely did it for Black Axe, he will be treated like a hero back in Nigeria. Basically, he will live like a king."

"Is it possible that once we know he is there, that we can we extradite him back here to Canada?" He asked.

"There are a few problems with that idea. The first problem is that I am not sure Canada even has an extradition treaty with Nigeria. But for arguments sake, let's assume we in fact do. The government of Nigeria is very afraid of Black Axe and the power they have, and I must say that this is for very good reasons too. We would have to prove he was there before the Nigerian police would even consider arresting him and then the courts there in Lagos would likely be paid off or the judges and their families might be threatened so that after the hearing, they would find him innocent and we would be unable to get him back to Canada to face our charges. Sorry Steven, there is little we can do from here. But we will be contacting the Nigerian embassy anyway. Who knows? I could be completely wrong, but I am not holding my breath, that's for sure."

With this new information obtained, a representative of the Attorney General's office went to the Nigeria High Commission in Ottawa for a meeting with their respective representative. In addition, the Interpol agency was also contacted about this murder and the organized crime behind it. Normally Interpol does not concern themselves with a single murder, but in the case where the accused is an active member of a world-wide criminal organization, they would certainly be a little more interested in this special case. Also, it is likely that Interpol already had extensive files on Black Axe.

It was only a few days later that Steven learned about the results of Attorney Generals' meeting with the Government of Nigeria itself. The Nigeria High

Commission in Ottawa assured the Canadian authorities that they will take strong action on this matter, but no one in the Canadian Government in attendance at that meeting seemed to believe that there was much that they could realistically be doing. Back in Nigeria the notorious group 'Black Axe' simply wielded too much power and control, usually through intimidation, violence, and even murder. If someone there was fortunate enough to be paid off, they had best cover their backs or they would be the next target, by either the authorities or by Black Axe themselves. For civil servants caught in this mess, they were dammed if they do and dammed if they don't. It was a no-win situation, but most would rather face the law in Nigeria than the torture and death handed out by Black Axe.

With this information, it was obvious to all of them that Abeo would get away with his crime. But at least they could all take comfort in knowing that he would likely never reappear in Canada at any time.

Robert even joked that being forced out of Canada back to some countries might be worse than being in a Canadian prison. Considering all that Canada has to offer, that statement carries a fair amount of truth to it. But when Abeo would be treated like a king there, it didn't seem fair at all. To Steven it was a double-edged sword. Abeo could not come back to Canada, which was good, but at the same time he would be living in comfort.

The Black Axe group had so much power in Nigeria, mostly because those who enforced the laws were afraid of possible repercussions from them. It was not unheard of for the family of law enforcement, officials, and even judges to be targeted. Who would want to put their own family in harm's way for a crime not even committed in your own country? The intimidation created by Black Axe was simply too strong for any real justice to occur.

Chapter Ten

Steven's work continued as normal in Prince George. A couple months had passed since Steven had completed his first year since graduating from Depot in Regina. He was doing well in his work as a general duty officer and knew that it would not be long before he would be off to a new detachment or posting, likely within the same province. He looked forward to what new adventures his career would lead him in.

On this one particular day, Steven was coming in to work in the morning when he checked his email and discovered a message from Paul in Toronto. Paul had advised him that he had learned through his contacts that there was a position with Special I in Ottawa, and that he had already sent them a letter telling them the details of what Steven had done and how he thinks Steven would be a good fit for their team. So, with this information, Steven felt that perhaps this is something he should pursue.

Steven previously had his resume and his CV all prepared and ready to go as his first year as a constable right out of depot had already come to an end. So, learning about this position and armed with the information for the opening in Special I in Ottawa, he applied for this posting right away. He also took some time to call Robert too. He asked him if he would consider being a reference for him in this opening. Robert said he was pleased to do it, but Steven found out that he went even one step further and actually contacted the Ottawa Special I office and personally recommended Steven to them as well. Robert likely knew exactly who to call in Ottawa for passing on a good word about Steven. With these two excellent recommendations backing his application up, Steven got the interview he had hoped for.

Steven may have been surprised at getting the interview, but no one who was aware of what he had accomplished in his first year as a constable, were surprised at all. They all knew that his work was good, and his inquisitive mind let him to search deep into an otherwise simple file. This led him from what seemed as a average suicide call to what turned into a world-wide criminal organization. So, everyone who knew his accomplishments were sure he would at least get the interview, everyone but Steven. He had his doubts, but in the end, he was told he was one of the candidates.

The interview was done over the phone. Steven was hoping for another flight, this time to Ottawa, and to have a couple days off, but considering how the interview went, he was not in the slightest bit upset by it. Besides, a flight to Ottawa was an unnecessary expense to the taxpayers of Canada, and Steven recognized and appreciated that fact. He had no idea what to expect during their questions, so he could not really prepare for the interview, but the questions they asked all seemed like ones he could respond too without any real difficulty.

It was during this interview that Steven learned that it was very unusual for a member of crown counsel to call up and recommend someone, it was even more uncommon for a member of RCMP Criminal Intelligence Program to put their neck on the line by recommending an RCMP member into the Special I section. Even if it was for a position in a completely different province and Robert was very near his retirement. There has always been a reluctance to put your neck on the line in case the person didn't end up fitting in with the team the way they hoped the person would. So, with having these two recommendations along with the reasons that they gave the interviewing panel, it presented Steven in an excellent light.

The interview consisted of the panel from Special I, asking the usual routine questions about the things he has done since getting into the RCMP. And then there was the detailed questions about his investigation of a break and enter that turned into so much more. The people on the other end of the phone seemed very impressed with his resourcefulness in getting the information that he needed in order to come to the conclusions that he ended up with. They were not even concerned with the fact that he contacted a friend in local electronics shop to get some information on how to trace email IP addresses. If anything, they seemed to appreciate how he gathered the information using his own initiative. Of course, the Special I team did have their own computer experts on staff too. But working from a smaller area such as

Prince George, he managed to get the information he needed to get the job done.

So, by the time the interview was over which was close to one and a half hours long, Steven felt good about it. It seemed like approximately fifteen or twenty minutes of this interview was the others on the panel simply asking questions around learning more about Steven as a person. They wanted to know about his friends outside of work, what he liked to do in his off-duty time, and any associations he may have with clubs or other organizations.

Of course, Steven had no idea how well the other candidates applying for the same position did in their interviews, but at least he was satisfied with his performance and the answers he had given during his time. He knew that even if he did not get the position, he did very well, and it was an achievement simply to get the interview with this section, as most who apply do not. Everything else to him was simply a bonus.

One of the three other people on the phone conducting the interview talked about the two references Steven had even before the interview. He did sound very impressed with the recommendations that were provided to the panel. So now that the interview had concluded, all Steven could do was sit back and wait for the eventual results, and if unsuccessful, to get the feedback he would need for other positions he would be seeking within the RCMP. Steven had no idea how long he would need to wait though. From the time he put in his application to join the RCMP to the time he left for Regina Saskatchewan to attend Depot, was several months. But this would likely be a much shorter time frame. Probably just a few weeks, or so he believed at that time.

Fortunately for Steven, not even two weeks had passed when he received a response from the Ottawa office offering him the position with Special I. Naturally, he accepted the new job without the slightest bit of hesitation. Now he needed to pack his apartment up and prepare for his big move to the East and re-establish himself in Ottawa.

The RCMP owns a house located in Ottawa in the heart of the city that is used specifically for members who are new to the area and need time to find a permanent residence. Steven would be able to move right into this house for a few weeks until he got his own home sorted out. He had arranged for a moving company to place his belongings into a shipping container so they could be stored in Ottawa until he had his home ready to have his belongings moved into his future home. This shipping company had a contract with the government of Canada, so there was little concern for the care of his personal belongings. But even still, Steven was hopeful he would not need to be in the temporary location for too long as he desired to have his own home with his own possessions. Being a dog lover, his plan was to get a puppy as soon as he was able to do so.

It seemed like mere days, but it was only about one month later when Steven was moving off to a new city. Prior to that he had two parties to attend. The first one was at the family restaurant with his friends that he had made during his year in Prince George. The second party he attended was a going away party held by the members of his shift in the RCMP. Both parties made him realize how valued and appreciated he is by both his co-workers and his friends. He felt like he would really miss all the people he was leaving behind in Prince George.

Ottawa was a long drive from Prince George, and winter months were soon setting in, so ensuring that there were excellent winter tires installed on his truck, Steven left for the long drive to Ottawa while all his belongings left by container about the same time.

Fortunately for Steven, driving through most of the prairies the weather was good and the only real snow he saw on the roads was from Prince George to Edmonton at the higher elevations. Steven had been to enough motor vehicle accidents to know that in winter months it is critical that he drove responsibly the entire distance. Driving too fast for the weather conditions will make a bad accident even worse. But he was prepared in his vehicle; he carried chains for his tires plus enough emergency supplies for the unpredicted things that could happen. He was well prepared.

Although it has only been just over one and a half years before when Steven drove to Regina, he was still at awe about how immense this country really is. The drive across this land was like its own vacation to Steven. This time, driving East he was able to see Mount Robson and he was stunned at just how big it really is. At almost four kilometers altitude, the huge size of it was breathtaking when driving past. He felt that no photograph could ever capture the true size of this mountain.

Being out on the open road, even in this time of the year, was something he really enjoyed doing. In the prairies, seeing from horizon to horizon always impressed Steven. But this would be his first drive East of Regina. He was looking forward to seeing the new sites and traveling through Manitoba and Ontario. He wisely chose to start each day driving at around ten in the morning and continue later in the day. That way he would not have the morning sun in his eyes. Also, he felt like he could see so much more of the landscape, that is until the sun went down behind him in the evening.

A few days later, Steven arrived in what would be his new home city for the next few years, Ottawa. As he drove up to the temporary house in a nice part of the city, Steven reflected on all the events that led him here. He felt like a truly blessed man despite not knowing anyone in Ottawa yet. But he also knew that no matter where he is, he likely has many friends nearby, he just needs to meet them. Fortunately for Steven, the keys to this home were mailed to him a couple weeks prior, so he simply unlocked the door and walked in. It was furnished and there was a television in the living room, but no linen was provided. Knowing this ahead of time he had brought sheets, towels, blankets and a pillow with him.

The very next morning, Steven checked his personal email and was happy to have received an invitation from a group of men who heard from those friends of his in Prince George. They knew that he was new in town, so they gave him an invite out to dinner to introduce themselves to him and vise versa. Steven knew without a doubt, this would be a good move for him.

Meeting with them served to confirm that he now had some new friends that he would likely keep for as long as he was in Ottawa. The dinner was much like the ones in Prince George, good food and better company. These people would not even let him pay for his own meal at the restaurant. They took care of the bill and made him feel so welcome. He knew that they would support him when it was time to unpack his shipping container after acquiring his new residence.

Chapter 11

It was not long after Steven got all settled in at his new temporary home in Ottawa, the house that is owned by the RCMP, that he began his search for a more permanent abode. He considered his needs and attempted to determine if he wanted to rent an apartment and slowly save and search for a nice house or live with a tighter budget and look for a house right away. He was a dog lover and had every intention on getting a dog or two as soon as he had a suitable home and a regular routine laid down. He knew for sure that in time he would like to have a decent house with a good yard for his dog, but until then, the dog would be fine provided that it gets out for plenty of exercise. He liked larger breeds, and contrary to popular belief, they didn't require a big home, just plenty of walks and exercise to keep them happy. In fact, there are some large breed who are happiest staying inside their kennel with the door open when they slept as it was much like their natural habitat of a cramped den.

In addition to his new friends, Steven was also getting to know the members of his team at the Special I office in Ottawa. He felt like he was fitting in well with them and he liked them all. Still it can take some time to build the relationships that he would like. But that was just a matter of time and experiences together.

Outside of work, he did meet the group introduced to him from the men out west. He knew it wouldn't take long for this brotherhood to accept him and he would have many new acquaintances. They already welcomed him. He simply needed to put himself out there, but he was in the process of doing that once he arrived.

He showed up to work every morning at about seven thirty, even though his routine office days didn't start until eight. This gave him some time to look online for rental properties or houses that he could afford with the small down payment he scraped together during his first year of policing. Within two weeks he decided he would rent and live frugally for one to two years to save money towards a permanent home.

He missed his friends at Prince George, especially the 'motely crew of reprobates' he often joined for Friday night dinners. But he always knew when he first met them after arriving to Prince George, that their time together would be limited to the duration of his positing in that city. But they would be friends, or even brothers, forever. He just never thought he would end up in the nation's capital just over one-year later. He figured his next posting would likely be in the Greater Vancouver area.

One day about two weeks after his arrival in Ottawa he came across an advertisement by chance for a slightly smaller home for sale. This gave the illusion of a larger yard. Even though he was planning on renting, this might be a good purchase for him. So, he made the arrangements to go see it with the realtor. She showed him the property and he liked what he saw, so he put in an offer to purchase the home.

The offer was accepted, and he had a possession date that was only one month away. He knew he would need some time to re-paint the interior and do a couple minor upgrades before he had the shipping container brought over to move his belongings in. Many of the men he met at the dinner a few weeks before had volunteered to help with the painting and repairs. They figured it could all be done over a weekend. With that much assistance, they were likely correct on this. But there was still one month away before he would take possession of his new home. And a team of free assistants cost a premium in beer and pizza. But it was money that would be well spent. Besides, within this group were people who worked in many different trades so he felt the work will be completed with much care.

Steven had been in Ottawa only about one month when he came in to work and received a message about a phone call from his friend Paul Barker the crown counsel in Toronto.

"Hi Paul, its great to hear from you. How have you been doing?"

"Pretty good. Too much work as always though." Paul laughed.

"I bet; Sounds like nothing has changed then. I am still getting settled in at Special I."

"I have no doubt that there is so much to learn and catch up on to be part of the team, but I am certain you will do fine."

"Very true, and in addition I need to move into my new home too. But that will happen soon as well. I bought a house so you will have to make the drive sometime for my housewarming party."

"Sounds great. Listen Steven, the reason I called you, besides to say hello of course, is to tell you that there was an arrest made a few days ago at Pearson International Airport.

"Okay?" Paul clearly had Stevens attention now.

"The Canadian Border Services Agency (CBSA) have arrested this person initially under the 'Immigration and Refugee Protection Act' for having a forged document, to wit a fake passport."

"I am sure that happens from time to time."

"Yes, but this time it was very different. Typically, we hold them pending the return results from the fingerprinting. If nothing turns up, they go through the court system and eventually get handed over to immigration for deportation hearings. But this time something did turn up."

"You have my full attention;" commented Steven.

"Well, the persons fingerprints came back as Abeo Adesina." His bail was revoked, and he will be going to trial."

"That is excellent news. But why did he return to Canada knowing this could happen?"

"A great question. We will likely never know the answer to it though. But I am certain that he thought his fake passport was better than it was." Commented Paul. "Also, whatever brought him back to Toronto, was likely important enough to cause him to risk his capture.

"When will the trial be conducted?"

"It will not happen for a long time. He will be appearing in the Superior Court on Thursday for a fix date appearance. We might set a trial date then, but I don't even know if he is planning to plead guilty or if he will elect a jury or judge alone. To my knowledge he doesn't even have counsel yet. But he may have re-hired his previous one."

"Paul, thank you so much for letting me know this. Please keep me in the loop on this. Especially if he applies for bail and gets it."

"Oh, he will apply for bail, I would bet on that one. I doubt it will get granted due to him leaving Canada last time. But in case he actually does make bail, you will be the first to know."

With this, the two of them disconnected their call. For a few minutes Steven thought of calling Marylin to tell her the news. It had been a few months since he last gave her an update and returned her computer at the same time. He thought about it and decided not to bother her. It may bring up old sad feelings about her sister. Maybe if there was a conviction, he would reconsider calling her, but he would make that decision when the time came. And that could be a long time in the future.

Epilogue

This account was the true story of how my new friend Steven (once again a pseudonym I have assigned to him), came to be in the Special I section. When I was interviewing him for all the details in this book, the one thing he asked me more than once to do was to finish this book off by detailing how to keep yourself safe when you are online, specifically with romance scams. For general on-line safety, there are many resources out there that I would encourage the reader to review. But here in this book I am more focused on romance safety. Here in Canada, there have been several suicides that have resulted due to romance scams, and sadly too, some are children.

General internet precautions are always advisable for on-line safety. Such as all accounts having different and strong passwords. I must admit I am terrible at this one. I have used the excuse that there are just too many passwords for me to remember. And of course, it is advisable to change your password regularly. But I am also bad at this. We should all consider using a password manager. Additionally, we should use a good virus scanner, and firewall. But keep them both up to date. Also consider getting a web camera cover for your computer to assist against being spied on. Purchase and service your computer from reputable dealers only. And be careful when purchasing a second-hand machine. Never let people you do not know and completely trust use your cell phone.

Anyway, we know these points, now I will discus romance scams and how to protect yourself.

How to tell a scammer?

So, you are registered on an internet dating site and you have spent considerable time selecting a profile photo or two. You put in thought into what to say about yourself, wrote your bio, read it and re-read it a couple times to ensure you are attracting the right future partner. You might even enlist a friend to assist you in the descriptions, so it sounds just right. Now once you are satisfied with the profile, you decided to post it online and then wait so see who will click on it to respond.

Over the coming days or weeks, you get some attention, usually based on the photographs you posted. Sometimes you wonder if the person responding had even read your profile. But occasionally, you get a reply that appears like the person had put real thought into it. So, this piques your interest. You then read their profile and look at the pictures too.

You then proceed to read their profile and look at their photos. With any luck, the person and their profile will appeal to you too. So, what do you with this potential partner? You might be excited to start something, or maybe you are very cautious. Now a prudent thing to do is to tell if this person is a scammer or, are they in fact a legitimate person wanting the same things you do? Are their motives truly sincere, or are you their latest mark to separate you from your hard-earned money? Sometimes the scam isn't even about money. It could be for immigration to a better country that equates to a better life, or another notch on their bed post. Perhaps it is just to try and collect nude photos. You are never wrong to presume that all potential partners are scammers until proven otherwise.

    If you are getting messages from someone who could be a body double for the best-looking models (male or female), check their photo online. Do this before initiating any reply. Copy the photo they use when contacting you, then paste it into 'Google's Reverse Image Search' or other such search engines. If the image you saw in the advertisement or dating site is also an image used in social media under a completely different name, you know it's a false profile. If it is used in an advertisement of any sort, it is almost certainly false (there is a remote chance the person works as a model, but I doubt it very much). Also (And please don't be mad at me for saying this), if you are low to mediocre attractiveness, be warry of someone who is stunning looking. Chances are good that they are a scammer. Are there exceptions? Of course, there are, but why would you want to take that chance? It is true that some cultures don't place as much value on looks as others do, but do you want to gamble this way? Also, if you are still in doubt, or you have that little voice in your head telling you to be cautious, it would be very wise of you to listen to this voice. Often your gut feeling is correct when it says to be very careful. It is also important to remember that when you do the image search, if it does not find a match, it doesn't mean they didn't steel the photo from somewhere else. So be careful always.

Everyone wants the passion and excitement that a good relationship offers, this is especially true at first. Nothing feels better than to know that the person you are interested in is also equally interested in you and the two of you are embarking on a new adventure that may even lead to a lifetime of companionship. But watch how passionate they are. Is it a reasonable level of passion? It is true that some people feel emotions stronger than others, but these are still signs that should be observed by you for your own protection. Always remember that online-dating scammers are charming. That is how they operate. Charming people have a way of drawing us in. You should also remember that you are not stupid if you fall for a scammer, they know how to draw you in and are the most practised chat-up artists the world has ever seen.

You should always be careful when you met someone online who claims to have fallen in love with you too soon, especially before you have even met in person. Most wise people take things slowly and although there are some legitimate people who move quickly, in order to protect yourself, go slow as the scammers often try to rush you. These people will claim to have a special bond with you and may say that with you they think they have found their "soulmate". Another common line they may use is that they've "never felt this way before". The scammers may talk about your future together, including marriage and families—whatever they perceive as you wanting to hear.

A vigilant dater needs to remember to always be a little cynical, at the very least until you've met in person. If you want an external opinion, show some of the messages from this person to a trusted, smart, and impartial friend, and ask them to be honest with you. A good friend will provide an honest opinion on their views.

As English often isn't the first language of foreign romance scammers, their spelling and grammar might not be very good. But some of them can be very educated and may in fact speak several languages. So, something to watch for is their writing. Do they mess up their tenses? Punctuation? ARE THEY USING TOO MANY CAPITALS? Basically, their grammar and level of English should equate to the education they claim to have. I heard of one scammer claiming to be a Captain in the military (not unlike the case that Steven worked on). But in most militaries, you must have a university degree to be an officer. So, their English ability must be equivalent to someone with that level of education. When I was researching this book, I decided to create an ad from myself on a dating website. I did receive a response from one scammer who she claimed to be a physician in the US Army working as a dermatologist. When I asked her what her rank is, she replied that she was a sergeant. But that is not an officer rank, and you cannot be in the military as a doctor without being an officer. In fact, the working rank of a doctor would be captain or higher. So, she instantly proved herself as a scammer to me. When I called her out on this, she instantly blocked me on this site knowing full well that she would never get anything out of me.

Another thing to remember is that scammers sometimes work in teams, with several different people all hiding behind one of their many different identities (both male and female). This is especially true of the scammers from Africa such as Black Axe. So, if your online correspondent's writing style seems to be strangely inconsistent, be very suspicious, if the education they claim they have does not fit their position, questing this to yourself is a good idea. Read every message and email with a discerning eye and not just the content.

Another common method that scammers employ is to express their desire to move things off the dating site. They may claim that their membership is about to expire, or that they are having log in problems. I say—tough. Until you've met in person, ALWAYS communicate only through the website you met on, and don't give out your real address, email address or phone number for some time, if ever. Most of the good online-dating sites have customer care staff that will investigate customer reports of unusual behaviour. The dating site can also check individual profiles and watch them specifically for any unusual activity (such as someone sending the same message to 50 or more people). Scammers don't want you to be protected, so they'll always encourage you to move away from the websites and onto personal communication as quickly as they reasonably can.

Probably the biggest clue that you are talking to a scammer is that they likely want money (but not always). If it is a scammer, at some point you will almost certainly receive a request for money (although some scammers are not there for money, some want citizenship, nude photos, or sex). In the case of a financial scammer, it might take weeks or even months to occur, but it will arrive. With the request will be a sad story and depending on the story, how long you have been chatting, and how strong your emotions have become, it will be interpreted as a real legitimate request. And you will always feel bad for saying no. But you should still ALWAYS SAY NO TO THEM, I can't emphasize this enough. If they are mad at you and say things like "obviously you don't really care about me or you would help me out." You know right away that at the very least, they are not the one for you, but it is more likely than not, that they are a scammer. My suggestion is to just block them from the dating site right away. Maybe even consider reporting them to the webhost. After all, the webhost wants a good reputation for the services they provide.

Does your online romance seem like they are not picky enough? Online-dating scammers are the least picky people on the planet. Statistically I am told that most legitimate men search for women at least five years younger than themselves, and usually closer to 10. Women usually search for partners around 2 years younger, to up to 12 years older. Of course, some cultures are less concerned with age differences, but I would suggest you still watch this as a possible red flag. With scammers, the sky is the limit. Be suspicious of men and women whose profile says they're open to contact from people 20 years or more away from their own age. Keep in mind that they are not open minded to age, these people are liars. They are trying to cast their net as wide as possible as the only thing they usually want is money (sometimes nude photos and other things – I will go into that later). Another good thing to do is to only date people who live close to you (no more than thirty minutes away). Most scammers live abroad, so they develop an elaborate cover story for that: Probably the most common one is that they claim to be in the Armed Forces, followed by the fact that they are or working overseas, or less common, engaged in secretive missions they can't discuss. If you receive a message from someone in another country, say you'll look forward to hearing from them when they're back here for good. It is almost certain you will never hear from them again. Don't be fooled by the photo of them that looks really good. The reason most claim to be in the military (whether they claim to be male or female) is because most people appreciate and respect soldiers for what they do. Also, there is the built-in excuse of why they can't get home or to keep their victim worried about the dangers of a war zone. As I am a retired soldier, I can tell you that it is true that women really do love a man in uniform (that is how I met my wife). Try to look at the person, not the clothing they are wearing.

One piece of advise I received when I was a young (and single) man that I feel is worth telling to all people when they go on a date in person whether they met on the internet or not is this: When out in public, observe how your date treats other people like servers, taxi drivers, ticket agents at a show or coffee shop staff. This will reflect who they really are. A date will almost always try to impress you, but the way they treat others tells you what you really need to know.

Some are looking for an easier life in a new country. Who can blame them? There are certainly some who will stay for life with their new partner, so long as they are treated well. Unfortunately, there are also some who as soon as they obtain permanent residency will leave their new spouse. This can cause heart ache at the least, and this is after potential thousands have been spent to have the partner moved here from their previous country. Flights to and from that country add up, but the real expense is in obtaining the legal right to bring their new partner to their country. It is also worth noting that you are legally responsible for this person. This means that the estranged spouse cannot go on welfare or other government assistance. You will be paying for that for possibly many years. I am not suggesting that it is wrong to marry a foreigner and bring them to your country, I am simply pointing out the concerns you should consider.

So, the person you have been chatting with has now passed all the scammer tests so far, and you are both anxious to finally meet. For personal safety you should agree to meet at a public place such as a coffee shop. The best time to do this is in the mid afternoon so that you still have a few hours of sunlight left. Daylight times are always the safest. You may want to consider taking public transit, so the other person does not see your car or decide to follow you home. It is best not to take a ride home if it is offered to you. Later if things feel right, you may consider exchanging phone numbers and planning date number two.

What to do when you discover you may be scammed?

So now you have connected to a possible partner and you learn they are a scammer, what should you do? Maybe you already met this person over a coffee, or maybe they are still just online. If it is not too late, and you either lost a small amount of money, or hopefully no money at all, simply cease all conversation with them and block them from the dating site or email. Consider the small sum of money lost as a write off. Unfortunately, you will never see it again.

Now let's consider that you had lost some money to the scammer, the first thing you should do is right away is start to compile as much documentation as you can. Document anything that you can recall such as the emails that you have saved, text messages, and anything else that could be used to help discover who is doing these scams and to assist agencies to put a stop to it. Again, photographs can also be used to show that the person is a scammer. Also, sever all contact with that person immediately. Don't ever feel you owe them an explanation as to why you stopped contact. They do not deserve an answer. Then to be safe, change all your account passwords. If possible, do it from a different computer like a friends' home or a work computer. Do not use a computer from a library or from an internet coffee shop as there is no way of being certain that the computer there is not compromised. Changing the password will help in case the scammers have hacked into your computer. By using a different computer, they are not getting the new passwords through a possible covertly installed program on the victims computer. Run a good virus (and trojan) scanner on your computer. Actually, you should get in the habit of doing a scan at least once a week and a deep scan at least once a month. And it never hurts to periodically change passwords anyway. A password generating program can be useful too.

Who to report a scammer too?

Ideally, send all important details of the person to the online-dating site you met them on. If everyone reported the scammers, it would help to shut them down, and then it will help people to meet the legitimate people who are looking for love, not cash. If you were taken for any money, you should also notify the police and get a file number for your case. You may not need the file number, but if you do, you already have it. Also keep in mind that many police departments do not have an internet fraud section or are overwhelmed by the amount of work these frauds can create. It is a sad truth that only a few years ago, internet crime did not exist, (neither did the internet). But sadly, it sure does exist today, in abundance. But if the police department does not have a computer crime section, ask them where you should go, as they would farm it out too. The RCMP may not have this section within small detachments, but they certainly have them at the division level, and even if they are overwhelmed, insist on sending them the data anyway as they will look at it and who knows, you may have given them the key piece of data that they need to help put a dent in it.

Other romance scams (used for sex, money, etc.)

Another type of scam that is less obvious is the single date for sex scam whereby the person (male or female) may just be looking for one night of sexual bliss and nothing more. There is nothing wrong with this, nor is it a scam if everyone is upfront and honest about it. But when someone truly believes that the relationship will develop into a long-term romance, feelings will be hurt, and they will feel used, or worse, left with an unwanted pregnancy or disease.

Another type of dating scam is where one person is using the date for nothing more than a nice evening out and they have no intention of seeing the other person again. Usually this involves convincing the other person to take them to a higher end restaurant and paying a premium for a nice meal and drinks, once it is over, the person finds an excuse to leave right away. Of course, if the person paying is acting like a jerk to the other, there may be a very legitimate reason for him or her to want to leave. It is mainly for this reason that I suggest a coffee shop for a first date. If the person says to you that they expect so much more than simply a coffee as a first date, consider yourself very fortunate in learning early on what this person is really like. Any 'nice' person (rich or poor) will understand and likely agree with this approach.

Another type of scam that occurs is when someone online preys on others (often teenage girls, but anyone can be a target to these scammers) and usually through charm convinces them to strip or show body parts or do lewd acts on Skype. Later on, after their victim does what is asked, they then threaten to turn the video that they recorder on Skype over to their parents, school, post it on Facebook (or other social media), send it to friends, coworkers, bosses, etc. Unless a fee is paid, or further lewd acts for their enjoyment.

Sadly, there have been young ladies who have been threatened by some to the point that the victim has killed themselves over the shame they felt. Unfortunately, the only thing these victims have done wrong is trust the wrong person.

Obviously, education and prevention are the first steps in preventing these scams from occurring. But let's assume it is too late for that. The first thing you need to do is immediately suspend your account so it has been removed (you can go back later and reactivate it). Now do the same with all your other social media sites. Next you need change your work passwords (preferably from a different computer) and update your virus scanner and run a full deep virus scan. Ensure you have a firewall up and running, and make sure that you delete your cookies, clear your cache, and wait. At this point the chances are pretty good that you will never hear anything further from them. So, a few weeks later you can re-activate your social media accounts if you feel ready to do so. I would recommend no sooner than four weeks.

If the low life scoundrel demands payment or they will release these incriminating photos, DO NOT EVER send them any money. If you do, there is no guarantee that they will destroy the files (if they really have them to begin with) and they could come back for more money later. Also, by giving them money you are guaranteeing that they will do this crime again to another victim. The best way to stop them is to ensure that they don't make any money from you. Remove their profit and they will go away. Okay, so that is easier said then done, but it starts with the victim.

Most of us have heard of the 'Nigerian Prince' email scam. It is perhaps one of the longest-running Internet frauds and the subject of many jokes. Also called "Nigerian letter" scams or "foreign money exchanges," these typically start with an email from someone overseas who claims to be royalty. The fraudsters lure you in by offering a share of a huge investment opportunity or a fortune they can't get out of the country without your help. Then they ask you either for your bank account number so they can transfer the money to you for safekeeping, or for a small advance payment to help cover the expense of transferring the money. That's when they either take your payment and disappear, or worse still, drain your bank account. Many people laugh when they get these emails and wonder who could possibly fall for it. But the truth is that there are people who still do. If you send out fifty thousand emails, at least one will attract someone, and the occasional one is all you need to rake in the money.

It was determined through a study by an independent organization that the average victim of this type of scam ends up loosing on average $2133. If a single scammer sends out one hundred fifty thousand emails a day (automated of course), even when the bulk of these messages gets ignored, you can quickly see how this could become quite profitable to the scammer.

People fall for these scams because they present victims with an idea of how to get rich quick with very little work. First, these scams play on people's greed. Many times, the scam is set up in a way where victims are promised that they'll make a hefty financial profit without much effort,

The best way not to fall for these scams is to recognize them for what they are. These types of emails are typically unexpected and from an unknown sender. Some email providers may even automatically send these to your spam folder, but inevitably some will get through.

If this type of email does land in your inbox, don't send them money or give out your personal information to strangers, no matter how sad the story or enticing the reward. The best thing to do is just delete the email.

If you do fall for scams like these, remember that lots of other people have made the same mistake. Document it and report it to your local police. But do not expect that they can get your money back for you.

Coincidently, as I was writing this last chapter, I saw a segment of W5 on the television. I believe it is on YouTube and it is worth watching it. The segment was about Black Axe and the victims. Amongst many things I have covered in my book, they interviewed a psychologist who told the reporter that when a person is in love, their brain releases chemicals that can actually hide the area of their brain that would logically think through the actions of the scammer as well as the victim themselves. This tells me that anyone can end up a victim and it is easy to sit back and accuse the victim of being naïve.

Another aspect of the scam that was shown on W5 was that Black Axe has a website designed to look like a bank website. The contact person 'shares' with their victim the bank account number and password for log in so that they can show how much money they have and simultaneously build the trust. If they need to 'borrow' money from a victim they can create a storey about how they cannot access their account at the moment but show how they are able to pay it back soon, which of course never actually happens. The problem is that this website is completely fake and the person the scammers are pretending to be don't have this account or the money displayed.

I do not believe I have covered even half of the romance scams that are used on the internet. I have no idea how many there are, but I suspect new ones are being thought up all the time. Protect yourself. Keep your eyes wide open.

Coincidently just before sending this draft of my book to the editor, I had an opportunity to interview a lady who years ago sustained a serious brain injury from a motor vehicle accident. She is now about forty years old, but her maturity is that of a twenty-five-year-old due to her unfortunate injuries. She was telling me of her desire to meet a long-term partner with the hope of marriage. She also told me that she has issues of trusting people too much.

She too met a man online who claimed to be an American soldier in the Middle East. He told her how he adopted an orphan and was looking after him with the hopes of bringing him back to the United States, when his deployment was done. He told her that he needed money to do the legal work to bring this child home with him, and she 'loaned' him twenty thousand dollars.

I asked her if she had a photograph of him, and she sent me a picture of him in his uniform. I immediately entered the image into an app for searching images. The page that followed showed several people claiming to have either been scammed by someone posing as him or having attempted to be scammed by this image.

I had to tell her the bad news, but she took it very well and asked me what she should do with this guy. I advised her not to have any more contact with him as he was likely a good speaker and she was too trusting. She did agree with me on that point.

Later I found out that he sent her several emails wondering why she stopped communicating with him. Although I said to her that she does not owe him any explanations, she chose to confront him about his scamming ways. That is when he blocked her, and the problem ended.

Clearly when a person, or group of people target not only the average person, but those who are handicap and other issues, with no regard for them whatsoever, we are dealing with a form of life that cannot even be described as human. They are monsters of the worst kind.

Reprinted from 'The Globe and Mail'

(Published November 12, 2015 Updated March 22, 2018)

Canadian police say they are fighting a new kind of criminal organization. The signs began to appear two years ago: photos on Facebook of men wearing odd, matching outfits.

Then there were stories, even old police files, attached to the people in the photos: a kidnapping, a man run over by a car, brutal beatings over what seemed to be a small slight.

Mapping a secret criminal hierarchy for the first time is a rare kind of detective work. So, when two Toronto police officers and an RCMP analyst in British Columbia started documenting the existence of something called the "Black Axe, Canada Zone," they could not have predicted it would take them to funerals, suburban barbecue joints and deep into African history before they understood what they were seeing.

The Black Axe is feared in Nigeria, where it originated. It is a "death cult," one expert said. Once an idealistic university fraternity, the group has been linked to decades of murders and rapes, and its members are said to swear a blood oath.

Most often, the group is likened to the Mob or to biker gangs, especially as it spreads outside Nigeria.

An investigation by The Globe and Mail that included interviews with about 20 people found that "Axemen," as they call themselves, are setting up chapters around the world, including in Canada.

Like any criminal organization, it focuses on profit, police say. But instead of drug or sex trafficking, it specializes in a crime many consider minor and non-violent: scamming.

What police have also learned is that, when done on an "industrial" level as part of a professional global network, scams ruin lives on a scale they have rarely seen.

Two weeks ago, at a news conference attended by FBI officers, Toronto police announced they had taken part in an international crackdown on a money-laundering network through which more than $5-billion flowed in just over a year. Two local men charged with defrauding a Toronto widow of her life's savings will eventually face extradition to the United States on money-laundering charges, they said.

https://www.theglobeandmail.com/news/national/shadowy-black-axe-group-leaves-trail-of-tattered-lives/article27244946/

Manufactured by Amazon.ca
Bolton, ON